THE PREMIER GUIDE TO
Brecon Beacons
& THE HEART
OF WALES

Editor and Principal Writer
Miles Cowsill
Managing Editor
Trevor Barrett
Contributors
John Norris, C.S. Moscrop, Roger Stevens, Sue Parrott, Diane Russell
Photography
Wales Tourist Board, Brecknock Council,
Radnor Council, Lily Publications
Published by Lily Publications

All accommodation participates in the Wales Tourist Board's inspection scheme. If readers have any concern about the standards of any accommodation, please take the matter up directly with the provider of the accommodation, as soon as possible. Failing satisfaction, please contact the Wales Tourist Board, Development Services Unit, Brunel House, 2 Fitzalan Road, Cardiff CF2 1UY.

Published by Lily Publications, 12 Millfields Close, Pentlepoir, Kilgetty, Pembrokeshire, Wales SA68 0SA. Tel: (01834) 811895, Fax: (01834) 814484. ISBN 0 9517868 5 7.

Contents

THE PREMIER GUIDE TO THE BRECON BEACONS & HEART OF WALES is unique in that it is the only publication dedicated to these two neighbouring and spectacularly beautiful regions of the Mid Wales countryside.

As with all titles in the best-selling PREMIER GUIDE series, the emphasis throughout is on easy reading and quick reference. Which is why a word of explanation is due here to enable you to be sure of your bearings.

Brecon Beacons as used in the title refers to the area in and around the Brecon Beacons National Park (one of three national parks in Wales), from Monmouth in the east to Llandeilo in the west, Hay-on-Wye in the north to Merthyr Tydfil in the south. It is a particularly wild and wonderful landscape, and the publisher readily acknowledges that words and pictures alone cannot even begin to convey the true spirit of this vast wilderness.

The Heart of Wales is an appropriate and evocative term now used to promote the breathtaking countryside begging exploration in the scenic rural counties of Radnorshire and Montgomeryshire. Here you will discover such delights as the Elan Valley and the rare red kite, the old market towns of Welshpool and Rhayader, and elegant Victorian spa towns such as Llandrindod Wells and Builth Wells. The region is even blessed with its own railway - the Heart of Wales line - which runs between Shrewsbury and Swansea and is a leisurely and highly enjoyable way to appreciate the true natural splendour of Mid Wales.

This handy guide gives you all the information you need to make the most of both the Brecon Beacons National Park and the Heart of Wales. Attractions, places of interest, where to stay and where to eat, sports and leisure activities and facilities, maps, town plans, and a full A-Z of towns and villages: all of this and more can be found within these pages, which make for great holiday reading.

Look out too for the other value-for-money titles in the PREMIER GUIDE series. These cover Pembrokeshire, Cardiganshire and several other equally beautiful parts of Wales, and new titles are being added all the time. The current list is shown on the back cover.

So happy reading - and a very happy holiday.

Miles Cowsill
Managing Director
Lily Publications

3

BRECON

Brecon Beacons, a national park offering a landscape of green open hillsides, sheltered valleys and traditional market towns.

Exciting activities await you in this rural part of Wales including pony trekking, gliding, watersport and of course walking.

Attractions can be found in abundance, with many unique to the Brecon Beacons area; including a Whisky Distillery, a Showcave Complex and Shire Horse Centre and our very own Woollen Mill.

Comfortable accommodation is an essential part of any holiday. There is a selection of good quality hotels and guest houses, self catering and caravan and camping sites or for the more adventurous bunkhouse and youth hostel accommodation.

Outstanding water facilities can be found here. The Monmouthshire and Brecon Canal, Llangorse lake and for the fishing enthusiasts the rivers Usk and Wye are a must!

Nationally renowned events here include the famous Brecon Jazz Festival, the Hay Festival of Literature and for the most unusual of events Bog Snorkelling.

So, come and visit us and find out for yourself!

Brecon Beacons & Irfon Valley

"the very essence of Wales"

For a copy of our full colour brochure and accommodation list contact:

Tourism Section (LP)
Neuadd Brycheiniog
Brecon
LD3 7HR
Tel (01874) 611729
(24 hours)

Why a Visit to the Brecon Beacons is such an Uplifting Experience

As the Tourism Officer for the Brecon Beacons, I am of course unashamedly biased when it comes to any debate about which area of Wales is the most beautiful.

I say unashamedly because countless thousands of annual visitors to the Brecon Beacons National Park are just as lavish in their praise of it as even the most enthusiastic local could ever be.

The plain fact is that the region around the Brecons, which on its eastern side extends to the English border, is a landscape to inspire feelings of true wonder. High, flat-topped mountains, rising to almost 3,000 feet at Pen y Fan, stand like sentries over gently rolling hills, lush river valleys, sparkling lakes, dark forests, deep gorges and tumbling waterfalls.

As if these natural scenic wonders were not enough, visitors are served up with a veritable feast of other delights: the Monmouthshire and Brecon Canal, winding its way through the picturesque Usk Valley; fascinating historic towns such as Brecon, Hay-on-Wye and Llanwrtyd Wells; and a whole menu of special events and attractions, from the Royal Agricultural Show at Builth Wells to the Brecon International Jazz Festival.

And as this guide clearly illustrates, the Brecon Beacons is an ideal - and idyllic - base from which to tour magnificent Mid Wales.

One thing I can guarantee. If this is your first visit to the Brecon Beacons National Park, it certainly won't be your last. So we look forward to seeing you again - and soon.

J Lewis

JANE LEWIS
Tourism Officer,
Brecknock Borough Council

View from Mynydd Illtyd

The Brecon Beacons National Park

The Brecon Beacons National Park centred on the highest ground in southern Britain. Yet these mountains are no pinnacled piles of dark, craggy rocks. They are massive, sculpted forms like giants slumbering under a green and gold quilt.

The national park stretches 40 miles east to west from the Welsh border with Herefordshire, and 15-20 miles from the small country towns of Hay-on-Wye, Brecon and Llandovery, southwards over the mountains to the heads of valleys once alive with heavy industry.

The great natural beauty of the park arises not only from mountains and moorland: there are deep cwms, broad valleys, ancient woodlands and sparkling rivers; and traditional features which give it special character. In fact the park's landscape has evolved through the interaction of people with nature over thousands of years. Geology, wildlife, history, and farming and other human activities have all played a part in the creation of this unique environment.

The designation of it as a national park is official recognition that it is of the highest landscape quality, deserving both special protection and assured opportunities to enjoy it, whether through strenuous activities such as hill walking, or by relaxation - even sunbathing, weather permitting!

The National Park Authority cannot do much about the weather (indeed the atmosphere is really one of nature's scenic delights here) but it has the job of seeing that conservation and recreation are top priorities. Careful planning and sensitive management are needed to reconcile the proper demands of local communities for development of the area with its conservation. The Authority's staff include an ecologist, archaeologist and teachers as well as planners, a lawyer, landscape architect, wardens and administrators. Volunteers bring extra skills and marvellous enthusiasm to many practical tasks.

The help of visitors is also essential in caring for the area, especially as the land is mostly privately owned and many local livelihoods depend on it. So please follow the Country Code wherever your exploration takes you.

The Underlying Rocks

The main rock of the mountains is sandstone, which gives them and the valley soils their characteristic red colour. The sandstone was laid down by ancient rivers depositing sand in shallowing seas. Ripple marks can still be seen clearly in the rocks in some places. Great earth movements uplifted these deposits to form massive mountain chains. Since then, the forces of erosion have been constantly at work, wearing away all but the remnants we see today. The bands of rock visible on the steep northern faces of the Beacons show that our mountains are like the last fragments of a giant layered cake, most of which has already been devoured by time.

Pen y Fan and Corn Du are higher than the surrounding area because the more easily eroded sandstones are still protected from the elements by a cap of rather harder coarse sandstone and conglomerates: it is this that forms the distinctive flat top of these two peaks.

Not all of the park is sandstone. In the south there are bands of younger carboniferous limestone, millstone grit and coal measures. The start of the coal measures often marks the park boundary today, as mining scarred the landscape of the South Wales valleys.

The broadest outcropping of limestone is around the village of Ystradfellte, along the courses of the rivers Mellte and Hepste. A whole series of spectacular waterfalls has been formed

Black Mountains ~ Skirrid Fawr

as these rivers cut down through the limestone to the harder millstone grit. Because limestone is soluble in slightly acidic water, rivers in this area sometimes flow below ground, where caves and caverns have been formed over thousands of years. Scientifically, these are some of the most important natural features of the park. Coal measures come to the surface on the park's southern boundary.

You are never far from a textbook example of a geological feature. Dramatic cwms deepened by glaciers, the effects of freeze-thaw glacial moraines, and upland lakes, scree slopes, swallow holes and dry rivers can all be found here. It is a perfect place to appreciate some of the natural forces that shape the land.

Wildlife

Although many parts of the national park look wild and untamed, the vast majority of the landscape is in fact directly influenced by the activities of people.

All high land is grazed by sheep, and sometimes by ponies. This year-round grazing, combined with harsh upland weather, greatly reduces the diversity of wildlife on the exposed mountain sides. However, the cliffs and ledges which sheep cannot reach support a much richer flora, including some very rare arctic-alpine plants. These undisturbed ledges also provide nesting sites for ravens and carefully protected peregrine falcons. In some places, where it has been possible to reduce the grazing pressure, there are expanses of heather, bilberry and sheep's fescue. Birds of the uplands include meadow pipits, ring ouzels, wheatears, curlews, snipe, lapwing and the occasional merlin.

The natural tree cover of the park is oak (ash and sessile oak) - woodlands which support a huge range of plants and animals. Red kites need this kind of habitat for nesting, so that as their numbers in Mid Wales increase, they may return to nest in many parts of the park.

Unfortunately, some slopes have been thickly planted with sitka spruce and other foreign conifer trees for timber production. Although such plantations provide homes for birds such as firecrests and crossbills, they do not support anything like the diversity of wildlife found in the native woodland that they often replaced.

Farmland on the lower slopes, with its distinctive patchwork of small fields and carefully laid hedgerows, is home to another, more adaptable, group of plants and animals. One of the more unusual inhabitants here is the polecat. Buzzards are commonly seen over farmland, either soaring over the fields or watching from fence posts. Hedgerows rich with foxgloves, primroses, bluebells and stitchwort can be enjoyed along narrow lanes in late spring. The footprints of badgers and small mammals may be spotted by the sharp-eyed.

Llangorse Lake is the largest natural lake in South Wales but has lost some of the teeming wildlife for which it was known for hundreds of years; yet it is still very important for its flora and fauna. Sometimes birds disturbed at Llangorse find refuge elsewhere: the shallow end of Talybont Reservoir is particularly good for wildfowl, and large numbers of wigeon, pochard, teal and various waders can be found there in winter.

The main river of the park is the Usk, which is famous for its salmon and trout. The Wye flows along the eastern edge, and the Tywi forms the park's western border. Along these rivers and their many smaller tributaries are found dippers, kingfishers and grey wagtails, and at night elusive otters hunt along the banks.

History - and Prehistory

The park is rich in fascinating sites that chart its history from the Stone Age to our grandparents' day.

Remains of chambered long cairns - burial sites of Neolithic farmers - can be seen in the Wye and Usk valleys, the most accessible being beside the A40 on the north-west edge of Crickhowell. Bronze Age round cairns are high on many mountains, including the tops of the Beacons themselves. Enigmatic standing stones and stone circles from these times are found on moorland and lonely mountain passes, such as Maen Llia in Fforest Fawr.

Later, Iron Age hillforts were built on defendable high ground, some probably functioning as permanent social, religious and market centres for the surrounding area. Garn Goch in the west of the park and Pen y Crug on the outskirts of Brecon are both good examples of the period.

When the Romans invaded the area in the first century AD, they set up a series of military camps, the largest being Y Gaer, a few miles west of where Brecon was later built. Well-paved roads linked Y Gaer to other Roman camps, and remains of such a track (Sarn Helen) can be seen on Mynydd Illtud Common.

The Norman conquest of Britain left its mark a thousand years later as Norman lords established their power-base by building a series of small castles and attempted to subdue the Welsh. Remains of such Norman keeps can be seen at Bronllys, Crickhowell and Hay-on-Wye. In the far west of the Park, Carreg Cennen Castle changed hands many times, serving as both a Welsh and English stronghold in the turbulent thirteenth and fourteenth centuries.

The circular keep at Tretower, near Crickhowell, is another reminder of this unsettled period of history. However, the associated manor house of Tretower Court, one of the finest surviving medieval houses in Wales, is the product of the more stable fourteenth and fifteenth centuries.

The park's heritage of religious buildings includes humble but fascinating small churches, such as Partrishow and Llanddeusant, often dedicated to Celtic saints of the post-Roman era. There are also remains of important priories at Llanthony and at Brecon, where the former

Driving in the Beacons

Parc Gwledig

Craig-y-nos
Country Park
BRECON BEACONS NATIONAL PARK

on the A4067 Sennybridge-Swansea Road

- Over 40 acres of woodland, grassland, lakes and riverside walks
- Open every day from 10am (until a time varying with the season). Admission free.
- Visitor Centre with display and activity areas
- Groups welcome but must be pre-booked

Craig-y-nos Country Park,
Pen-y-cae, Swansea Valley, SA9 1GL
Telephone or Fax (01639) 730395

priory church became the Cathedral of the Diocese of Swansea and Brecon in 1923.

Perhaps surprisingly, there are many reminders of the early industrial revolution within the park boundary. Water power from the rivers was harnessed at an early date to run machinery, and wood was used in charcoal furnaces; coke later provided steam power, and limestone served as a flux in ironfounding. The most impressive remains are in the Clydach Gorge west of Abergavenny, and just south of the park boundary at Blaenavon.

The Monmouthshire and Brecon Canal is a reminder of the extensive system of horse-drawn tramways and waterways in South Wales which preceded the railways. They carried heavy raw materials and industrial products, and also brought lime into agricultural areas and took farm produce to markets in the expanding valley towns.

Museums in Brecon, Abergavenny and Merthyr Tydfil provide fascinating insights into local rural and industrial history of these times.

The Countryside at Work

Farming has determined the look of the Brecon Beacons National Park for hundreds - maybe even thousands - of years. The patchwork of fields and hedges, and the bare uplands, have all been shaped by the pattern of farming life.

Most of the upland areas are common land. This often misunderstood term does not mean that the land is owned by everyone. Common

The National Park Visitor Centre

Mountain Centre

There's no finer place to view the Brecon Beacons, enjoy wholesome refreshments and learn about the National Park.

BRECON BEACONS NATIONAL PARK

- Open daily from 9.30am. Admission free
- Information and exhibition about the Park
- Freshly prepared hot and cold meals
- Local moorland walks with panoramic views
- Special summer events programme (walks, craft, etc)

5 miles south-west of Brecon - follow signs from A470 or A40 to
NATIONAL PARK VISITOR CENTRE
Mountain Centre, Libanus, Brecon, Powys, LD3 8ER.
Tel (01874) 623366.

land belongs to a landowner in the usual way; what makes it different from an enclosed field or garden is that neighbouring farms have traditional rights in common to share use of the land. In practice this means that many local farmers have commoner's rights to graze sheep on the open mountains. This ancient farming system, which pre-dates the Norman conquest, only survived on the poorer high lands.

The most easily farmed valleys have been agricultural holdings for hundreds of years, and now provide improved grazings for sheep and some cattle, with hay, barley, silage and other winter feed crops are grown here.

Methods of farming have changed rapidly across Britain in the past fifty years. Locally, the trend has been towards larger farms and silage rather than hay meadows. Pastures have been ploughed up and re-seeded with rye-grass for improved sheep grazing. Traditional stone barns have often been replaced with much larger, prefabricated buildings.

As sheep subsidies are being reduced, many farmers are finding life difficult, and there is concern about the whole future of smaller family farms here. However, incentives are beginning to be introduced to encourage sound environmental management in farming, instead of rewarding ever increasing output.

Although sheep farming has dominated the park's landscape, other human activities have also left their mark. The high rainfall and steep-sided valleys made the area ideal for the creation of reservoirs. There are well over a dozen within the park, providing water for the populous valley communities to the south.

Many large catchment areas around the reservoirs, and other large areas of old woodlands or moorland, were planted with conifers for timber production by the Forestry Commission and private forestry groups. Many of the older blocks have reached productive maturity and are being felled. Forest Enterprise is taking this opportunity to re-design their forests, with more broadleaved trees, to the benefit of wildlife and landscape.

The park also contains a few active limestone quarries and a silica mine, and on the southern boundary opencast coalmining is encountered in a few places.

The Countryside for Leisure

In an increasingly busy and urban world, we all need a little beauty and peace. The Brecon Beacons National Park, perhaps best known for its fine walking country, offers many other opportunities for active or relaxing enjoyment of the great outdoors. Pony trekking is popular, and cyclists can also make use of the network of bridleways. Watersports include canoeing on the canal, sailing and windsurfing on Llangorse Lake, and fishing on rivers and reservoirs. Showcaves in the upper Tawe valley can be visited (even if caving elsewhere must be left to those with special skills and local knowledge); and nearby is Craig-y-nos Country Park, with over 40 acres of woodlands, water and meadow to explore.

Passions for bird watching, botany, archaeology and landscape painting can be indulged in many places. There are ancient monuments and countryside attractions to visit - from the narrow gauge steam railway to a forest centre and a rare breeds farm.

National Park and tourist information centres can provide more help and advice, but as an introduction to the National Park and all it has to offer, you cannot do better than go to the National Park Visitor Centre (the Mountain Centre) 6 miles south-west of Brecon. Admission is free, the views are superb, family walks and events are organised through the summer, and the tea-room serves very good food!

Roger Stevens

From Barn Owls to Motor Bikes
A Day with a National Park Warden

The Brecon Beacons National Park covers 519 square miles of some of the most magnificent scenery in Wales. The National Park Authority employs six Area Wardens (and one Assistant). You don't need an MSc in Applied Mathematics to work out that if you lose your way whilst walking in the Brecon Beacons you are not guaranteed to come across a helpful warden around the next corner!

So what do our wardens spend their time doing if they can't be relied upon to guide straying visitors? No day can be selected as typical, and the kind of work with which a warden gets involved may depend on the season, and also which part of the national park he or she (we do have female wardens) works in.

Let's take as an example a recent day selected at random from Sarah's weekly report. Sarah

Fishing at Crickhowell

works in the westernmost part of the park.

Her 'patch' consists of the Welsh-speaking farming communities along the fringe of the park and a chunk of wild and windswept hill land - Y Mynydd Du, the Black Mountain. The National Park Authority owns the Black Mountain, and Sarah's duties include liaising with the farmers who graze their sheep on this area of common land. Remember that most land within the park does not belong to us or is even in public ownership of any kind. It is owned by individual farmers, but again it's important for Sarah to know them .

Back to Sarah's day! It begins with a visit to her two Estate Wardens and their temporary helper who are working on a woodland site near Myddfai. The site is an ancient semi-natural woodland, mainly of oak and other broadleaved

varieties. It is part of a farm whose owners have entered into a management agreement with us. This involves a five-year programme of thinning out the oak trees to enable the ones left to grow on to maturity. Many of the woodlands in the park are no longer managed for their timber and are often simply used as additional grazing and to provide winter shelter for sheep. This frequently leads to the woods disappearing over the years. Because woodlands are an important feature in the landscape of the park and provide wonderful wildlife habitats, we try to encourage landowners to manage their woodlands positively. Management agreements such as this are beginning to show some of the benefits. Our Woodland Officer is negotiating with a charcoal maker to use the timber provided by the current thinning operation on this site - much more environmentally friendly than using imported charcoal for your barbecue! The farmer will also eventually gain from the timber produced from a well managed wood.

Satisfied with progress here, Sarah goes on to visit Llanddeusant, where the village school has sadly just closed due to falling numbers on the register. She hopes to set up a Watch club in Llanddeusant. 'Watch' is a wildlife club for children run by the county Wildlife Trusts. Several of our wardens are involved in helping out with their activities. Sarah's particular specialities include dissecting barn owl pellets to identify their food, and building homes for otters. These graceful nocturnal creatures are increasing in numbers along many of the rivers in the park. The provision of artificial 'holts' made from piles of logs provide resting and breeding quarters for them. This is a favourite project for volunteer groups, especially children who enjoy designing and building what sometimes turn out to be 5-star hotels for otters!

Sarah's day next takes her to a meeting with a member of staff from the Countryside Council for Wales. She needs to keep in regular contact with other organisations such as this. The meeting this time concerns a barn owl nesting site where there is a proposal for development which may affect it. The National Park Authorities of Wales and England, as well as being set up to promote conservation and public enjoyment of the countryside, are the local planning authority. The wardens do not get directly involved in planning or development control issues, but they keep an eye open for things which planning staff need to be aware of in their patch. The warden is often the first point of contact which local people as well as visitors, so on planning matters and others, though a warden may not know the answer to every question, they will always 'know a man who does' !

Sarah's day continues with a drive on to the Black Mountain to visit an area where we have received complaints about motorbikes being ridden on the hill. Sarah speaks regularly with the local police constable about such problems. No recent tracks are to be seen today. So she spends a while picking up litter from one of the car parks on our land, but will need to return another day to finish the job, perhaps with some of our volunteers. We have a willing band of about 250 individuals who volunteer their time cheerfully to help us with our work. As well as the perennial litter-picking, more constructive projects include planting trees and digging ponds. Many volunteers have 'adopted' footpaths and bridlepaths and survey them and report problems to us on a regular basis. They can also join in with one of our regular work parties, building stiles or bridges, or clearing vegetation. We also have volunteers who, together with the wardens, lead our guided walks or help with the programme of events at our visitor centres, or at local shows. They may be asked to build dry-stone walls, clear scrub from wetland sites and churchyards; or to adopt 'trig points' or even pubs - strictly for the public benefit! The range of projects is continually growing.

From Barn Owls to Motor Bikes

Sarah ends her busy day with a visit to Carreg Cennen Castle to discuss the filming of a short item on environmental education for a television series, possibly using the projects which she has done with the village school at Trapp. All our wardens visit the schools in and on the edges of their `patch' on a regular basis. They are involved in many ways - from helping the children to design and construct their own nature gardens, to helping the teachers organise field trips out into the national park, perhaps to visit some of the many archaeological sites. The wardens have the support of our Education Officer in this work, who is able to provide slides and artefacts on a wide range of subjects from `early peoples' to `water habitats'.

Had I chosen another warden or another day to write about, this short article probably would have been quite different! Each warden has special skills and enthusiasms which help shape their work programmes. For instance, Sarah has working sheepdogs, which she brings to special events such as our `farming weekend' held at the National Park Visitor Centre. Alan is our expert on hill navigation and map and compass work.

Mike is a geologist, and can be persuaded to `bodge' at some of our summer events (bodging is the traditional craft of turning wood on a home-made lathe). Bill has enthralled generations of schoolchildren with his gripping stories of the Romans marching into Wales through the national park. Gareth is a keen cyclist, keeps his vehicle in meticulous order and enjoys our woodland work. Clive is a local farmer's son, so there's not much he doesn't know about hill farming life. And anyone who has had a conducted tour around the waterfalls area with David will appreciate the width and breadth of his local knowledge.

So, enjoy your visit to the Brecon Beacons National Park. You may or may not meet the wardens, but there are reminders of their work wherever you go: stiles and waymarks to ease your journey, or woodlands, dry-stone walls and ponds to improve your view! But don't forget that the most important people in the park are not the wardens but the farmers and other landowners who care for the countryside 365 days a year.

Sue Parrott

Black Mountains

The Monmouthshire & Brecon Canal

One of the many delights of the Brecon Beacons National Park is the Monmouthshire and Brecon Canal, which runs from Brecon to Newport. The 'Mon and Brec', as it is commonly known, was originally two canals.- the Monmouthshire and the Brecknock & Abergavenny - which joined end to end at Pontymoile, near Pontypool. The Monmouthshire section is itself not without interest but lies outside the area covered by this guide. By contrast, the Brecon and Abergavenny section lies almost wholly within the Brecon Beacons National Park, hugging the mountainside for much of the way as it follows the River Usk through beautiful scenery on its course to wards Newport.

Leaving Brecon, where a feeder from the river supplies the canal with water, the canal is at first on the north side of the river, with views across it to the Beacons At Brynich the canal descends by a single lock before crossing the river on a massive four-arched aqueduct. A wooded section immediately above the river gives way to open countryside and final views of the Beacons before the canal moves toward the villages of Pencelli and Talybont. Drawbridges add interest along this section, culminating with an electric drawbridge across a busy minor road at Talybont. An embankment carries the canal though Talybont and past the wharf where the Brinore tramroad constructed by Sir Benjamin Hall (of Big Ben fame) brought coal and limestone to the canal.

The 375 yard (340 m) long tunnel at Ashford soon follows. To the left there are fine views across the Usk valley to Allt yr Esgair and Buckland Hill as the canal skirts Tor y Foel. At Llangynidr the canals drops down through a sequence of five locks, the top three in an attractive woodland setting. Meandering and

river-side sections are followed by splendid views across Glan Usk to Myarth Hill and then Pen Cerrig-calch, with 'table mountain' set on its eastern flank. After Llangattock, where lime kilns are a reminder of the tramroad from the Llangattock escarpment, fine views of Pen Cerrig-calch slowly give way to Sugar Loaf.

Gilwern, in the parish of Llanelly, was once one of the busiest spots on the canal. The tramroad constructed by the B&A Company brought coal down to the canal from collieries in the Clydach valley and at one time sixteen boats a day carried coal towards Brecon and intermediate coal yards along the way. Other tramroads for the iron trade followed. Govilon wharf, now the headquarters of the Govilon Boat Club and the location of the British Waterways canal manager's office also had tramroad connections. as did Llanfoist. An evocative picture of the industrial scene at the latter, now so quiet and peaceful in its beautiful setting against the wooded hillside is painted in Alexander Cordell's gripping novel *Rape of the Fair Country*.

After Llanfoist the canal rounds the head of the majestic Blorenge and there is soon a subtle change in the nature of the canal. Impressive views towards Abergavenny and the two Skirrids recede to give open views over the Usk plain. The villages of Llanellen, Llanover and Penperlleni are bypassed, though only a short walk away, as the canal keeps on the higher ground necessary to join the Monmouthshire. The canal has a more isolated and lonely character, though none the less attractive for that. This is briefly enlivened by the boating activity at Goytre Wharf. Below Goytre the feeling of solitude is even greater until from Mamhilad onwards traces of industry and housing begin to draw near. Throughout the length of the canal, pubs offering food and real

The Monmouthshire & Brecon Canal

Peaceful canal scene

BEACON PARK BOATS

Cruise the beautiful Monmouth and Brecon Canal in the Heart of the Brecon Beacons National Park. Our fleet of luxury narrowboats and wide-beam boats is at your disposal. This canal is a delight to explore and is never crowded, even at the height of the season.
Write or phone for colour brochure to
Beacon Park Boats, The Boat House, Llanfoist, Abergavenny, Gwent NP7 9NG, Tel (01873) 858277.

ale are never far away.

The canal has something to offer almost everyone, whether country lover, boater, walker, angler, or industrial historian. Handsome trees - oak, beech, sycamore, ash and sweet chestnut among them - share the banks with the ever present alder. Springtime primroses, violets and celandines are followed by reed mace and yellow flag, rosebay willowherb and foxgloves. Cherry blossom, rhododendron blooms, buddleia and rowan berries add their touch in season. Wild raspberries, elderberries, blackberries, hazel nuts and chestnuts are among the fruits available for the picking.

Every season of the year gives the canal a different face, and a winter's morning with the sun sparkling on frost-dressed trees is as attractive in its way as the colours of autumn or a golden summer's morn. The trees provide habitat for many common garden and woodland birds, among them tits, wrens, woodpeckers, nuthatches and treecreepers. Swallows swoop low over the water in summer; siskins feed on the alder cones in winter. Herons are a common sight at the water's edge and buzzards may often be seen over open countryside towards Brecon. For the lucky or the observant, the brilliant blue flash of the kingfisher is a treat.

Ducks - both mallards and 'bitzas' - grace the canal at many points; moorhens are often to be found where there are reed beds. Frogs and toads are common, and mink are all too often to be seen; correspondingly rare are the water voles. Pondskaters rush about on the surface of the water in summer and damsel and dragonflies dart above it. For the angler with an NRA rod licence, a variety of coarse fish - roach, dace, perch, bream, gudgeon, and mirror carp among them - await beneath the surface. Fishing rights along much of the canal are let to angling societies, but there are also unrestricted sections. Details of these, and the necessary fishing permit, can be obtained from the British Waterways office at Govilon Wharf.

For the experienced boater the navigable section, just over 34 miles in length (55 km), may seem short. Certainly it is possible to rush up and down the length of the canal in a few days at bank-damaging speed and see nothing. However, the discerning will find plenty to fill a week, while the 'energetically-challenged' will find that the small number of locks and the 23-mile-long lock-free pound from Llangynidr to Pontymoile - one consequence of the decision of the B&A promoters to keep their canal at high level instead of descending by a series of locks to join the River Usk at Newbridge - will suit them too.

Boats for weekly or part-weekly hire may be had from bases at several points along the canal - Goytre, Llanfoist, Gilwern, Llangynidr and Pencelli. Day boats may be hired at Goytre and Talbont. For those wishing to enjoy the restfulness of the canal to the full, there are the alternatives of a cruise on a trip boat from Brecon, a horse-drawn boat from the canal museum at Llanfrynach, or a week on a pair of hotel boats.

For the visitor, the canal is accessible at many points, but car parking is not always easy. Convenient parking points include the British Waterways car parks at Goytre and Govilon. The width and quality of the towpath vary, but improvements at several points, including Brecon, Gilwern and Pontymoile, have made the path more suitable for those in wheelchairs. Apart from the pleasure of following the towpath itself, other walks that use lengths of the towpath include the Usk Valley Trail, the Taff Trail and signposted local walks at Brecon, Llanfoist and Govilon. Cycling on the towpath is not permitted, but there is good cycling country around the canal and mountain bikes can be hired from the Venture Centre at Talbont.

Popular vantage points for motorists who want to view the canal with minimal walking are Brynich lock (parking available nearby in a layby with telephone box on the A40) and the locks at Llangynidr (limited parking on the bank

by the bottom lock; alternatively in the Coach & Horses car park for patrons only). Boating activity at the locks is greatest early and mid-week and quietest on Fridays and Saturdays.

For the historian the canal, now a picture of peace and tranquillity, is a fine piece of 'liquid history'. The horse-drawn boats, approximately 63 ft long by 9 ft 6 in wide, crewed by a man and boy, and carrying up to 25 tons of cargo, have long gone and the once noisy wharves now see only pleasure boats. But for those with eyes to see and imagination to conjure with, there are buildings, tramroad remains and other relics of the past to evoke the scene as it was, when tens of thousands of tons of coal, lime and limestone, iron and other cargoes were carried on the canal each year. A visit to the Water Folk Museum at Llanfrynach will prove an entertaining and informative aid to visualising the past.

Both the Monmouthshire and the Brecknock & Abergavenny canals were largely the work of one engineer - Thomas Dadford junior, one of the family of canal engineers responsible for a number of canals in Wales and the English Midlands. The main line of the Monmouthshire was completed in 1796; the Brecon & Abergavenny took rather longer. The Gilwern to Brecon section was completed early in 1801, but there was then a delay. The coal and lime trade towards Brecon was initially more important to the Brecon & Abergavenny Company than the iron trade towards Newport, and it was not until 1812 that the canal company minutes were at last able to record "The Committee set out to view the Canal towards Pontymoile and at Mr. Waddington's Boat House in Lanover, met him, and embarked there on board his Boat, and proceeded in the same all the way from thence to, and through, the Stop Lock at the Junction into the Monmouthshire Canal - being the first entrance from this Canal into that - amidst the acclamation of a very numerous body of the inhabitants as a token of their Joy at an Event so very beneficial to this Country."

Monmouth & Brecon Canal

Viewed through the eyes of the many local shareholders, the two canals were a poor investment, partly because a toll-regulating clause in the B&A Act of Parliament for goods passing through to the Monmouthshire Canal encouraged ironmasters to lay tramroads to both canals, forcing the canal companies to compete and reduce tolls to barely economic levels. Trade was at its best in the 1820s and even then dividends on the B&A never exceeded 2.5%. Dividends slowly declined until railway competition all but killed trade in the 1850s.When the Monmouthshire (by now the Monmouthshire Railway & Canal Company) took over the B&A in 1865, shareholders received only £25 for their £150 shares. In 1880 the joint concern was taken over by the Great Western Railway.

In a wider sense the two canals were indeed a success. Together with their associated horse-drawn tramroads, they provided a transport network vital to the exploitation of the mineral resources of the region, linking quarries, mines, ironworks and limekilns with manufacturing, agricultural, export and domestic markets. Prices fell and the availability of coal, lime, manufactured products and agricultural produce improved. Immense riches fell on wealthy landowners like the Duke of Beaufort, whose royalties on coal, iron ore and limestone extracted from his mountain land in the parishes of Llangattock and Llanelly (Gilwern) increased thirty fold in twenty years. Some of the wealth trickled down to those at the bottom end of the scale and the wealth and prosperity of the region as a whole rose.

Most of the Monmouthshire Canal is at present unnavigable. Some of it lies culverted beneath Cwmbran; in other places bridges have been flattened. However, much tidying up and local restoration has taken place, parts are still 'in water' and most of the line can still be followed

on foot. The Crumlin arm, which leaves the main line at Crindau, at the north of Newport, is well worth following to the Fourteen Locks Canal Centre and impressive flight of derelict locks, weirs and side ponds at Rogerstone. Two lengths that have been restored to navigable condition are a short length at Gwastad, on the outskirts of Newport, and the most northerly two miles approaching Pontymoile. Reconstruction of the culverted Crown Bridge at Sebastopol, essential to the latter length, was carried out by Torfaen Borough Council in 1994, assisted by grants from the EU, the Welsh Development Agency and Gwent County Council.

The entire Brecon & Abergavenny Canal, save for a short infilled final piece at Brecon, is navigable. It owes its survival largely to its continued use as a water feeder, long after through navigation had ceased in the 1930s, and to restoration by British Waterways in 1970. The cost of the restoration was jointly borne by the Monmouthshire and Breconshire County Councils through the Brecon Beacons National Park Committee.

John Norris

The Wildlife of Brecknock

Take a little portion of Snowdonia, a dash of the Lake District and a pinch of Exmoor. Add to this a sprinkling of ancient woodlands, a carpet of old hay meadows and a wild swathe of the Flow Country. Apply them all to the 400-million-year-old foothills of central Wales and you have a recipe for the beautiful landscape of Brecknock.

The old county of Breconshire, which today makes up the southern portion of Powys, can be geographically divided into three main areas.

The north is dominated by the Cambrian Mountains, a wild upland plateau resounding with the "too-ee" cries of golden plover and the bubbling songs of curlew. The bleak landscape is carpeted by purple moorgrass, heather and bilberry. Running off the hills, the waters have carved narrow and steep-sided valleys, often cloaked with slow-growing oak woodlands, above a blanket of mosses and lichens. These can best be experienced in the Elan Valley Estate and the RSPB reserve on Corngafallt.

This is red kite country at its finest, a rich mosaic of woodlands, fields and hedgerows. Magnificent maiden oaks, some over 200 years old, provide suitable nesting sites, and the steep valley sides generate the up-draughts of air upon which the kites glide in search of their prey.

The 20th century has been a hard time for the red kite: in the 1930s the population was reduced to a couple of breeding pairs. Numbers have increased since, but only slowly. Infertility brought about by inbreeding, the effects of pesticides and persecution, and changes in land management practices have all had an effect. In the face of such adversity it is wonderful that kites now number over 100 breeding pairs in Wales.

The mid part of Brecknock is similar in characteristics, but very different in use. Much of

Peat Pool ~ Cribarth Hill

Mynydd Eppynt was cleared of its farming heritage 50 or so years ago to provide for a military training ground. In many respects the landscape has been fossilised as a result, revealing a countryside as it was moulded by early 20th-century farmers, farming by and large without the aid of internal combustion engines. Many of the fields are small and surrounded by banks and walls. Some even show traces of ridge and furrow farming. The range is now shared by the military and sheep from neighbouring farms.

Access to the range is generally restricted to two roads. On any visit look for wheatears, which characteristically bob and bow on rocks and posts or dart from one to the other in search of insects. The most numerous bird is the meadow pipit, which unfortunately is the main prey item for the elusive merlin, which can sometimes be seen flying rapier-like low over the ground.

The third, most southerly and most spectacular of the three areas of Brecknock is that within the Brecon Beacons National Park. The park itself contains three distinct ranges:the (Carmarthen) Black Mountain or Mynydd Ddu, the Brecon Beacons central plateau (comprising Fforest Fawr and the Brecon Beacons themselves), and the Black Mountains. Rising to nearly 3000 ft, Pen-y-Fan is the highest of the peaks and is the dominant feature of the scenery.

The principal rock formation is of old red sandstone, laid down over 400 million years ago. To the south, this is overlain by carboniferous limestone and millstone grit. These are two very different rock types which make for an interesting juxtaposition of vegetation types, the former being alkaline in its influence and the latter acidic.

All three are Palaeozoic rocks and were formed during long periods when seas and brackish waters covered the land. The different rock types arise from the variety of materials which settled out of the water, be they sand, the remains of corals and shellfish, or quartzites.

Purple moorgrass and matgrass are the dominant vegetation types, but cottongrass, heather and bilberry grow where the peat is deep. The lower slopes, however, are characterised by tall stands of bracken. The more exciting vegetation is often to be found in the more inaccessible places, such as crags and cliff faces. On the precipitous northern faces, Arctic-alpines such as purple saxifrage, and plants like sea campion and roseroot, can be found. The plant communities are little changed from those which colonised the land immediately after the last Ice Age had shaped and scoured the rocks 10,000 years ago.

Buzzard and raven are the commonest of sights, but careful searching will reveal ring ouzel in the screes, or golden plover occasionally on the moors. Peregrine nest on the more inaccessible rock faces.

Flowing between and alongside the three upland massifs of Brecknock are the rivers and tributaries of the Usk and Wye. These rivers have carved deep channels, both narrow and broad, in the landscape. The valleys are lushly clothed in vegetation, mainly grazing pasture for sheep, but where the sides are steeper grow rich broadleaved woodlands and large conifer plantations.

The rivers are teeming with wildlife. Both the Usk and the Wye are famous for their salmon and trout fishing, and fish of this calibre only survive where the waters are relatively clean and the insect life abundant. Herons, kingfishers and dippers are also plentiful, although they are not so common in the upper reaches of river where acid rain wreaks its damage.

In some of the tributaries the crayfish can be found, its population as yet unaffected by the more aggressive American species which have colonised some British rivers, and apparently free of the crayfish plague which has decimated numbers elsewhere.

On an evening walk near open water between April to October, you are likely to see bats flitting in and out of the trees and swooping low over the water as they catch insects. Stretches of the towpath of the Monmouth and Brecon Canal are a flurry of activity at dusk. A bat detector will pick up the noise of their echo location signals and reveal the identity of the species, which is not easy to do with the naked eye in the fading light. If you can catch a glimpse of a pale underbelly as it skims the surface of the water, this will be Daubenton's Bat.

The creature everybody wants to see is the otter. The Usk and the Wye are strongholds for this rarity, but such was not always the case. Here as elsewhere the population of otters crashed alarmingly in the 1950s and 60s. The intensification of agricultural practices brought farming right up to the river banks and removed

Brecon Beacons from Penderyn Road

many of the bankside trees which provide cover and homes for otters. In addition, the rivers were polluted with the pesticides which escaped from the land. The pollutants did not always kill the otters, but they caused reduced fertility and prevented successful breeding. The otter is a shy animal, easily disturbed, and its activity is now almost entirely restricted to the hours of darkness. But in the quieter stretches of river it may be possible to catch a glimpse of an otter at play during the daytime.

Mink are abundant, and not just along the main rivers. Seemingly bolder, these smaller cousins of the otter can often be seen vigorously searching the roots, nooks and crannies of the riverbanks. With care the two species can be readily distinguished. The mink is about half the size of an otter; at about 12" long it is more closely related to the weasel. An otter is nearer the size of a fox or small dog. In addition, the mink generally has black fur and the otter brown.

It is possible to distinguish them in the water too. The mink is positively buoyant, floating like a cork with much of its body out of the water. The otter on the other hand swims with almost all of its body underwater. Once out of the water the mink appears bedraggled, its fur drenched. This is because it lacks the stiff guard hairs which, in the otter, trap air close to the skin.

As well as the rivers and tributaries, the landscape boasts over a dozen large waterbodies, most of them man-made reservoirs storing drinking water for south east Wales. There is, however, one natural and very special body of water - Llangorse Lake, or Llyn Syfaddan. Llangorse Lake is one of the most important in Wales and was designated a Site of Special Scientific Interest in 1954 on account of its rich botanical heritage. Although over a mile long and half a mile wide, the average depth is only about 6-8 ft. The lake lies in a kettle-hole - a depression left in the land when permafrost and ice in the soil melted after the last Ice Age.

Llangorse Lake is unusual because of a combination of factors. The shallowness allows plants to grow throughout much of the lake. It is also eutrophic, which means that it is rich in nutrients and therefore highly productive for plant life. This in itself is unusual because the surrounding land or catchment is small in area, has little human population and low agricultural intensity. Chemically the lake is quite alkaline.

The vegetation is abundant and rich, and in places exhibits a pattern classically resembling that of successional processes. Ecological succession theory has it that shallow open bodies of water are colonised by floating-leaved plants. These are succeeded by emergent vegetation such as reeds and yellow flag iris. As the reedbeds dry out, they are invaded by alders and willows, forming a damp woodland or carr. Hence there exists a succession from open water to woodland. Behind the woodland, the unimproved fields are rich in varieties of marsh and spotted orchid.

The lake is also one of the most important sites in Wales for birds. It has the sixth largest reedbed, which in turn provides home for the second largest breeding colony of reed warbler (numbering up to 200 pairs). The reedbed provides refuge also for water rail, sedge and Cetti's warblers, and hundreds of roosting martins and starlings. Great crested grebe, coot and mallard all breed on the lake, building their nests in the quieter areas away from boating and fishing activities. Careful management of the fields has led to the return of breeding lapwing.

During the spring and late summer all kinds of "exotic" species may be observed. Ospreys are regular visitors, passing through on their way either to the breeding grounds of Scotland or the wintering quarters in Africa. Black terns and little gulls are also seen from time to time.

Of the reservoirs, Talybont is the most

Maen Lija ~ Prehistoric Standing Stone

rewarding. It is near to Llangorse and probably provides safe refuge for many species when the recreational use of the lake gets too intense. Talybont reservoir is also a Site of Special Scientific Interest, and a local Nature Reserve. Its southern end is most worthy of a visit, for it is quite shallow and resembles the lake in many ways.

Another man-made legacy providing valuable habitat within the landscape is the conifer plantation. There are large tracts of forestry, several of which grow alongside the reservoirs. Although much maligned by many, these plantations provide the necessary conditions for a wide variety of species which would otherwise be absent from the area. Undoubtedly the increasing number of hobbies which return each year from Africa to feed on swallows, martins and dragonflies, is a result of this mosaic of habitats. More residential though are the goshawks found in some of the secluded areas. They feed mainly on grey squirrels, but the odd pheasant or sparrowhawk does not escape their dinner table. Just occasionally come reports of crossbills, and another species more usually associated with the forests of Scotland, the pine marten.

The first grey squirrels reached Brecknock in 1949; until then our native red squirrels were quite widespread. Today the last reds hang on in the large plantations of Mid Wales, finding there a refuge from their more aggressive American cousins.

In the newly harvested areas of plantations, two peculiar summer visitors can be heard more often than seen, especially at night. The grasshopper warbler and the nightjar both make strange churring calls which carry over long distances. The warbler is rarely seen, but the nightjar might be, quartering low over the ground at dusk and resembling a cuckoo in flight. During the day it sits tight on the forest floor, its plumage providing perfect camouflage.

The broadleaved woodlands vary according to location. Mostly they are oak woodlands rich with mosses and lichens, grasses or flowering plants. In the areas of limestone, ash is the major component, often with a dense understorey of hazel, and rare plants such as lily of the valley. Another speciality of the limestone is the whitebeam, of which there are three species found nowhere in the world other than perilously perched on the craggy cliffs in Brecknock. Alder woodlands grow in the damper areas and birch can be found higher up the slopes in the Brecon Beacons.

The woodlands are not as intensively managed as they once were. Even in the 1950s, large areas would be coppiced - a method of cutting down trees which allows them to regenerate naturally with lots of stems. Often this provided fuel for local iron-ore smelters, or charcoal. The bark, especially of oak, was also valuable to give the tannins essential material for treating leather.

In spring the woodlands are alive with the songs of warblers. Chiff-chaff, willow warbler and wood warbler can all be recognised with a little practice. Other species more often seen than heard include the pied and spotted flycatchers, and the redstart. The latter's rufous tail is unmistakeable and is usually all that is seen as the bird disappears into the undergrowth.

Farming is the mainstay of the local community. Centuries of little - changed practices have yielded a patchwork quilt of small fields bounded by hedgerows and woodlands. This provides an ideal habitat for the sparrowhawk, the fox and the badger. Polecat, too, thrives in this kind of environment, but persecution, pollution and habitat change have reduced its population to the Welsh borders.

In a habitat such as this, with rabbits, sheep and plenty of small mammals, it is small wonder that buzzards are present, and in large numbers. There may be well over 500 pairs of buzzard in the area and few journeys are not blessed with the sight of a buzzard wheeling, circling and gliding in the sky, calling with that familiar "mew".

For most people the enduring memory of a visit to the area is of the buzzard and its graceful flight. The scenery is beautiful - the rugged uplands of the Brecon Beacons, the rolling foothills, and the lush valleys of the Wye and the Usk - but the next time you think of Brecknock will be when you see a buzzard.

Diane Russell

BRECKNOCK WILDLIFE TRUST

The Brecknock Wildlife Trust is a registered charity and it relies on its members and supporters to carry out its work. The Trust owns or manages twenty Nature Reserves, conducts surveys and monitors species, and provides advice and information as well as working with schools and providing a programme of talks and guided walks. You can help the Trust by becoming a member. Please join now and for a modest Annual Subscription, you will be helping protect the wildlife in this beautiful part of Mid Wales.

Brecknock Wildlife Trust, Lion House, Lion Yard, Brecon, LD3 7AY (01874) 625708.

*G*o to the people who really know Wales for your holiday information. The Wales Tourist Board produces a series of publications covering everything from castles to craft shops, car touring to narrow-gauge railways.

The Castles and Historic Places Guide, for example, covers more than 140 sites.

Then there's the best-selling series of information-packed Visitor Guides to South, Mid and North Wales, which tell you everything you want to know.

And don't travel around without a copy of the popular Tourist Map.

For copies, call in at a Tourist Information Centre, local bookshops or newsagent, or contact Wales Tourist Board, Distribution Centre, Davis Street, Cardiff CF1 2FU Tel (0222) 499909

THE BEST GUIDES COME FROM THE WALES TOURIST BOARD

BWRDD CROESO CYMRU
WALES TOURIST BOARD

Waterfall Country

At its northern end, the beautiful Vale of Neath extends into the foothills of the Brecon Beacons National Park. This is known as waterfall country - famous for the number and variety of its spectacular falls, which are unique in Britain and much admired for more than two centuries by a succession of artists, poets, writers, photographers and now film makers too.

The best-known and most accessible falls are those at Melincourt and Aberdulais, as well as the seventeen enchanting cascades created at Gnoll Country Park, Neath, by Herbert Mackworth in 1740.

Many more waterfalls are to be found in the wooded valleys and deep gorges of the rivers Mellte, Hepste and Nedd, between the villages of Pontneddfechan and Ystradfellte, on the southern

Black Mountain

edge of the Brecon Beacons. The only way to see them is on foot, and the car park of the Angel Inn in Pontneddfechan is the ideal starting point.

The easiest of the walks from here is to the falls at Sgwd Gwladus. It takes about 45 minutes each way along a marked footpath, and the lower sections are negotiable by pushchairs. The walk is also suitable for the less able.

Some of the other eight falls in the area can be more difficult to get to, however, particularly in wet and slippery conditions. So it is well worth referring to two very useful publications, both of which should be available from the Tourist Information Centre in Pontneddfechan.

One is the full-colour booklet Waterfall Walks in the Vale of Neath, and the other is the Brecon Beacons National Park leaflet Waterfall Walks in the Ystradfellte Area. Also essential to the serious waterfall explorer in the Vale of Neath is the Ordnance Survey Outdoor Leisure Map Number 11.

The nine falls in the Pontneddfechan area are Sgwd Gwladys and Sgwd Einion Gam on the River Pyrddin; Horseshoe Falls, Lower Ddwli Falls and Upper Ddwli Falls on the Neddfechan River; the Sgwd-yr-Eira Falls on the River Hepste; and the falls of Lower, Middle and Upper Clungwyn on the River Mellte.

Each is spectacular in its own way, and if revisited at different times of the year, rewards you with new aspects of its natural beauty as the changing seasons alter the face and colour of the landscape.

Enjoy your holiday in Brecon & the Heart of Wales!

The borough of Dinefwr (pronounced Din-ev-oor) was created as part of local government reorganisation in 1974. It is an area of 374 square miles, encompassing some of the most beautiful countryside in Wales, and it lies to the west of the Brecon Beacons, touching the counties of Dyfed, West Glamorgan and Powys.

Dinefwr takes its name from the medieval castle sited on a rocky outcrop in the Vale of Towy, just a mile or so west of the market town of Llandeilo - the administrative centre of the borough, and once the county town of Carmarthenshire. There are two other towns in the borough - historic Llandovery and the more industrialised centre of Ammanford - and the majority of Dinefwr's 40,000 population live within these three towns.

Dinefwr has been described as the gateway to ancient Wales. It is a region of spectacular landscapes and Welsh culture, with a history so shrouded in the mists of time that it has become indistinguishable from folklore, myth and legend.

Dinefwr Castle was built in the 12th century. It was the stronghold of Rhys ap Gruffydd, who successfully resisted the English invaders until Edward I brought the struggle to a violent conclusion at the end of the 13th century. During the reign of Henry VIII, the descendants of Rhys moved out of Dinefwr Castle and into Newton House, a stately home nearby. Rebuilt in the 17th century, this is now owned by the National Trust and is being restored; part of the ground floor is already open to the public. The castle itself is owned by Dyfed Wildlife Trust and is being

Brecon Beacons - Carmarthenshire

repaired by Cadw to allow safe public access.

Dinefwr Castle is not the only magnificent medieval stronghold still surviving in the borough. One of the most dramatic is Carreg Cennen Castle, perched high on a rocky limestone crag 300 ft above the River Cennen. A few miles away is the hilltop ruin of Dryslwyn Castle, which stands within clear view of Paxton's Tower, a 19th-century folly. The town of Llandovery also has its castle ruin, overlooking the town's car park.

This is an area where you can find your own space: there are over six acres of countryside to every inhabitant - a fact readily apparent as you take in the sheer majesty of the scenery. The Cambrian Mountains rise to the north of the Vale of Tywi, while brooding to the south is the Black Mountain of the Brecon Beacons National Park. Birds of prey circle high above the landscape, among them the once-threatened red kite.

The Black Mountain, the Cambrians and the valleys of the Tywi and Cothi rivers are now the subject of signposted tours, designed to entice motorists off the beaten track. This is the way to discover the real Wales, taking you past such dramatic sights as the Llyn Brianne Reservoir - a man-made lake holding more than 13 billion gallons.

Helping to preserve the natural beauty of Dinefwr is a novel scheme called Tir Cymen (meaning Tidy Landscape). Under this scheme farmers receive a special payment to protect landscape, wildlife and archaeology, with extra incentives to preserve features such as ancient woodlands and field boundaries. Dinefwr is one of only three districts in Wales to be selected for the scheme.

Other great visitor attractions of Dinefwr are the Roman gold mines of Dolaucothi, near Pumpsaint, which are owned by the National Trust, and Gelli Aur Country Park, near Llandeilo, where you can enjoy a day exploring nature trails, a deer park and the famous arboretum.

Dinefwr

Dinefwr - A land of myth & legend which is a treasurehouse of Welsh culture & history.
Its spectacular scenery includes areas of the Cambrian Mountains, Brecon Beacons National Park & the Towy Valley.
The market towns of Llandovery & Llandeilo are ideal centres from which to tour much of west & mid Wales.
Enjoy a warm Welsh welcome in this unspoilt corner of Wales.

Discover its Secrets

For Further Information Phone 01558 822521 Ext 268
or write to Tourism Officer, Dinefwr Borough Council, 30 Crescent Road, Llandeilo, Dyfed. SA19 6HW

Dinefwr is also noted for one other feature: its concentration of traditional Welsh craft workshops and studios. For example, in Llandeilo a co-operative known as Crafts Alive stocks hundreds of hand-made creations, both practical and decorative, and up river in Llandovery the former Meat Hall has been transformed into a new craft centre. In addition, the Trapp Arts & Crafts Centre has a shop and display area within its workshops. Many local artists and craftspeople also extend a warm welcome to visitors who wish to see them at work in their premises.

Further information about any of Dinefwr's many visitor attractions is available from the Borough Council's Tourism Office in Llandeilo. Ring (01558) 822521, ext 268.

Ammanford

Until the late 19th century, the Cross Inn at the centre of Ammanford was almost the only building here. The town developed quickly because it is situated on the anthracite coalfield, and although the landscape is dotted with coaltips the surrounding area is not an industrial wasteland, as there is a great deal of agricultural land and some beautiful scenery. Good views are afforded from a main road that runs over the Black Mountain to the Tywi valley.

Llandeilo

A Tywi-side market town standing in rich farming land, Llandeilo is a fine centre for fishing and for touring the many castles in the area. The 19th-century stone bridge over the river measures 365 ft in length and has a central span of 145 ft. Originally of the 13th century, the church is dedicated to St Teilo and was virtually rebuilt in 1840. Inside are two Celtic cross heads dating from the 10th or 11th century. Ruins of

Dinefwr Castle lie one mile west and overlook the Tywi valley. These ruins are near a privately-owned castle which was built in 1856 on the site of a Tudor house. Golden Grove mansion lies south-west and has been rebuilt. This was once a residence of the Vaughan family, whose members have played such an important part in Welsh history, and is now the home of the County Agricultural College.

ATTRACTIONS & PLACES OF INTEREST

The Trapp Art & Craft Centre

It was back in 1987 when Nigel and Julie Card decided to convert the old barns at Llwyndewi Farm into a craft centre. Time has certainly proved that the idea was a good one. It is now one of the leading independent craft centres in South Wales. The combination of art gallery, craft shop, exhibitions, craft demonstrations and coffee shop has been much appreciated by both local residents and visitors alike. The shop has a predominately 'made in Wales' theme with crafts from all over the principality. The art gallery has a truly magnificent selection of original and limited edition paintings, many of which are the work of local artists.

Llandovery

This market town is at the top of the Tywi valley, surrounded by hills and unspoilt country. The main street has a small square with the Market House in the centre and next to it a curious structure with a clock tower. Nearby is the Black Ox Inn with memories of the days, in the late 18th and early 19th centuries, when Llandovery was an important centre of the droving trade. The great herds of black cattle were collected here, to be driven over long routes on the hills to the cattle markets of England. The drovers were the first bankers of rural Wales, and the Bank

Church in Brecon on the rugby field, is one of only two public schools in Wales. It is a building in the gothic style and was founded in 1848 by Thomas Philips, who wished the Welsh language to be the basis of the education.

Llandovery stands at the junction of several roads. The road to the east, towards Brecon and the Usk valley, runs through a deep, wooded defile. The road to the south follows the fertile Tywi valley to Llanwrda and Llangadog, from which the route goes over the Black Mountain. The road due north follows the Tywi to its source in the wild country around Llyn Brianne. The north-east road takes the same course as the railway into central Wales. The railway crosses a high viaduct at Cynghordy and then tunnels under the pointed hill of the Sugar Loaf.

of the Black Ox issued its own notes. Llandovery is still very much a modern-day drovers' town on market days, with the busy stockyards crowded by farmers in the shadow of the castle ruins.

There are two notable churches in the town, both situated outside the centre. The parish church of Llandingat, to the south, was restored by W D Caroe in 1913. The church of Llanfair, about one mile north of the town, stands on a high, tree-clad bluff and was also restored by Caroe - who seems to have been in sympathy with the feeling of antiquity that the church imparts - and he salvaged rather than rebuilt the structure. A fine medieval tie-beam roof covers the nave, and the chancel has a barrel roof. The walls of the building are extremely thick, and the windows appear to have been placed quite haphazardly. There is modern glass in the east window and in the south side of the chancel. The grave of William Williams, Pantycelyn, the great hymn writer of the Methodist Revival, is in the churchyard.

Llandovery College, a big rival of Christ

Sports & Activities
in the Brecon Beacons

Where better to enjoy the great outdoors than in the wonderfully stimulating environment of the Brecon Beacons?

Walking, climbing, abseiling, pony trekking and gliding are just a few of the many sporting and recreational activities which help draw visitors to the area in such large numbers.

The following is a brief alphabetical guide showing the variety of excellent sports and leisure facilities available in and around the Brecon Beacons National Park. For a more extensive list, contact the appropriate Tourist/National Park Information Centre as listed on page 143.

GLIDING IN THE BRECON BEACONS

Black Mountains Gliding Club

Talgarth is the UK's premier ridge, wave and thermal soaring site. The airfield location provides more and stronger soaring conditions all year round than any other gliding site in the British Isles.

The club do not usually fly unless it is soarable. In 1990 they flew and soared 285 out of the 364 days available; on average the two-seater flight time is 45 minutes. This allows beginners much more flying time and, as a result, faster learning progress than is normal at the average gliding site.

It is usual for beginners to expect two flights

Sugar Loaf

or more per day, up to one hour in duration, though this may be modified to suit prevailing conditions and availability.

A fixed fee is charged for the course, and flying is charged in two parts - the launch and soaring time. An average week will cost £250-300.

Holiday courses are normally run Monday to Friday all year round. We limit the number of pilots on a course to four per instructor to ensure maximum individual attention and the best utilisation of soaring conditions.

The club operates two to three two-seater sailplanes - K13, Blanik, IS30 and IS32 plus one single-seat SZD 51-1 Junior. Launch is by 235 hp PA25 Piper Pawnee.

All our instructors are highly experienced at flying Talgarth and will be only too pleased to offer help and assistance in any soaring aspect.For further information telephone 01874 711463 or 01874 711254

GOLF

Brecon Golf Club

Newton Park, Llanfaes, Brecon. Tel: 01874 622004

Builth Wells Golf Club

Golf Club Road, Builth Wells. Tel: 01982 553296

Cradoc Golf Club

Penoyre Park, Cradoc, Brecon. Picturesque 18-hole parkland course designed by C K Cotton in 1969. Situated two miles north of Brecon off B4520 in Brecon Beacons National Park. Full catering and bar facilities available daily. Visitors welcome. Further information telephone 01874 623658.

HORSE RIDING

Hill Valley Riding Centre

This Centre is situated in the picturesque Brecon Beacons close to the village of Llangynidr. The proprietor, Jim and Elaine Christopher specialises in catering for families and small groups, and welcomes the novice rider as well as the accomplished rider. Instruction is provided for those who require it, and we are happy to help all to build confidence and improve their riding skills. The Centre is registered with the Wales Tourist Board and is approved by the Wales Trekking and Riding Association. For further information telephone 01874 730841

Tregoyd Riding Centre
Three Cocks, Brecon Tel: 01497 847680

OUTDOOR PURSUITS

Black Mountain Activities.

This company is based in the Wye Valley on the edge of the Brecon Beacons National Park, in the village of Glasbury-on-Wye.

The centre was set up in the early 1990s by two enthusiastic outdoor pursuit instructors, Carl and Hugh Durham, who between them hold a wealth of experience in mountaineering, canoeing and caving, gained at home and abroad. The centre has been approved by the British Canoe Union since the start, and has been an accredited centre since the introduction of the Wales Tourist Board's Centre Accreditation Scheme in 1993. All staff hold the relevant national qualification of the pursuit in which they lead.

Black Mountain's clients come from all over the British Isles, ranging from individuals, schools, youth and social groups to large blue chip British companies. Courses are individually designed for each group, from covering just one activity on a specialist course to a multi-activity

week. For further information contact Black Mountain Activities on 01497 847897.

Mountain and Water

Evocatively-named Mountain and Water is a business whose aim is to promote enjoyment of the countryside and great outdoors through a variety of relaxed activities.

Launched in 1987 by Pam Bell and Phil Swaine, this unique enterprise offers courses, field studies and other activities led by experienced instructors who share a common love of the Brecon Beacons and its landscape. All instructors are graduates qualified in disciplines such as environmental and earth sciences, and they will be happy to share this knowledge with you. For further information ring 01873 811887

Talybont Venture Centre.

The centre runs a wide range of outdoor group activities and management development courses, including mountain bike hire (helmets, toolkits and routes provided), caving, abseiling, activity days (river crossings etc) and gorge walking. There is also a shop specialising in outdoor clothing, mountain bike accessories, maps and local information. For further details telephone 0187 487458

SWIMMING POOLS

Brecon Leisure Centre
Penlan, Brecon. Tel: 01874 623677
Ystradgynlais Indoor Swimming Pool
Maesydderwen Comprehensive school, Ystradgynlais. Tel: 01639 844854

Builth Wells Indoor Swimming Pool

The Grove, North Road, Builth Wells. Tel: 01982 552603 or 552324

Sennybridge Indoor Swimming Pool

Sennybridge School, Sennybridge. Tel: 01874 636512

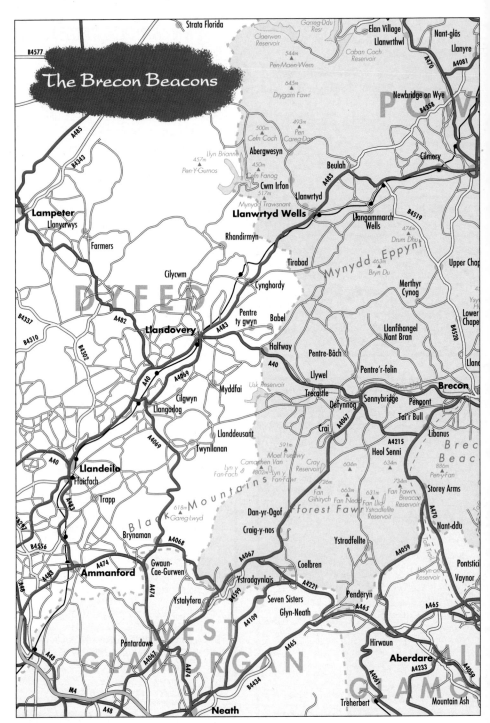

The Brecon Beacons

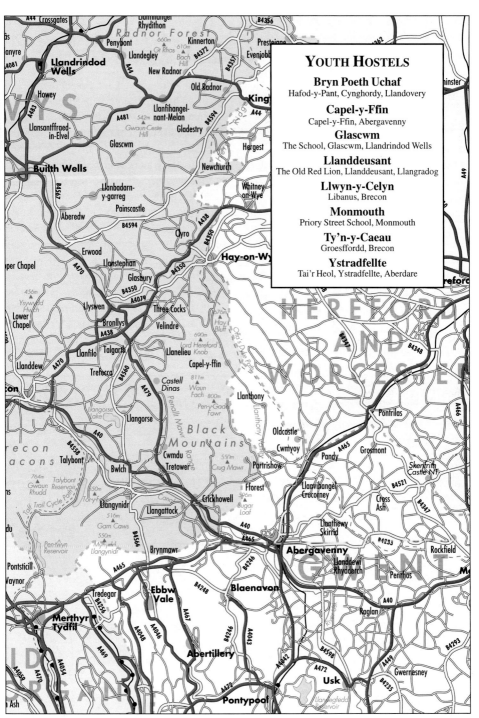

YOUTH HOSTELS

Bryn Poeth Uchaf
Hafod-y-Pant, Cynghordy, Llandovery

Capel-y-Ffin
Capel-y-Ffin, Abergavenny

Glascwm
The School, Glascwm, Llandrindod Wells

Llanddeusant
The Old Red Lion, Llanddeusant, Llangradog

Llwyn-y-Celyn
Libanus, Brecon

Monmouth
Priory Street School, Monmouth

Ty'n-y-Caeau
Groesffordd, Brecon

Ystradfellte
Tai'r Heol, Ystradfellte, Aberdare

A ~ Z of the Brecon Beacons

Abergavenny

This busy market town is held to be the gateway to Wales, and is the entrance to the Brecon Beacons National Park. To the north is Sugar Loaf (1,950 ft), an extinct volcano, and north-east is Ysgyryd Fawr, on which are the remains of a chapel dedicated to St Michael. To the south-west, Blorenge (1,832 ft) is a good viewpoint. The beautiful River Usk flows just to the south of the town and runs roughly parallel to the Monmouthshire and Brecon Canal. The Romans had a fort here and the foundations of this are thought to lie under the castle mound.

The castle was founded by Hameline de Balun early in the 11th century. It was captured in 1215 by Llywelyn the Great, extensively damaged during the Glyndwr uprising, and destroyed by parliamentary forces in 1645. The few remains date from the 13th and 14th centuries and consist of two broken towers, the gateway, and fragments of wall. The interesting town museum is situated in the castle grounds.

Abergavenny's main street contains buildings from many periods. Especially noteworthy are the 19th-century Angel hotel, which was an important coaching inn, and the gothic-revival town hall. Other interesting buildings in the town include the 16th to 17th-century King's Arms Inn; the early 19th-century King's Head Inn and adjoining medieval arch; and the Old Court, a house dating from 1500 built into the old town walls. St Mary's Church in Monk Street is the town's most important piece of architecture. Originally it was the church of a

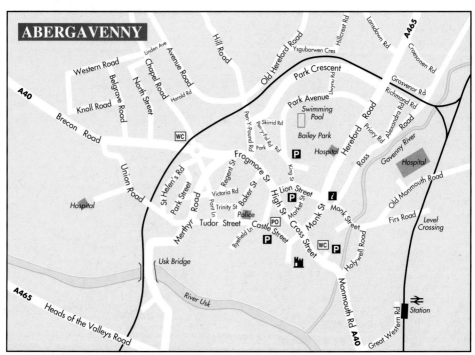

Abergavenny

Benedictine priory founded in the 11th century, but today only the tythe barn and prior's house remain of the priory buildings. The church contains many treasures, including 24 choir stalls dating from the late 14th century and a huge wooden figure of the patriarch Jesse in the Lewes chapel. Several fine tombs dating from the 13th to 17th centuries can also be seen in the building.

The road (A465) four miles north of the town passes the ancient hamlet of Llanfihangel Crucorney, under the slopes of the Skirrid. Here the Skirrid Inn, the oldest in Wales, has retained its medieval construction.

Nearby is the Tudor mansion of Llanfihangel Court, with a beautifully furnished interior. Charles I was entertained here during his unhappy visit to Wales in the final stages of the first Civil War. It is open occasionally during the summer months.

ATTRACTIONS & PLACES OF INTEREST

Abergavenny Museum

The Castle, Castle Street. Tel: 01873 854282

Abergavenny Castle

Castle Street. Tel: 01873 854282

Hill Court Gallery

This independent gallery is privately owned and directed. Contemporary paintings and artists' prints of professional quality are always on show. Exhibitions change every two months and provide the chance for established artists and promising newcomers to show their work for enjoyment and possible purchase by visitors. Entry is free during exhibitions every day except Mondays 2.30 to 7.00 pm.

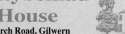

Blaenafon

Coal mining and iron dominated this town in the past; today they still play a role, as the local coalmine and ironworks are open to visitors. The Big Pit, which closed in 1980, is now open to visitors as a museum. The workings of the former coalmine are intact and accessible, and there is also a mining gallery which illustrates methods of coal extraction, as well as an underground guided tour at the mine conducted by ex-miners. Blaenafon Ironworks, opened in 1789, is also open to visitors. The blast furnaces and workers' cottages can be viewed at this historically important site.

ATTRACTIONS & PLACES OF INTEREST

Big Pit Mining Museum
Tel: 01495 790311

Blaenafon Ironworks
Tel: 01495 792615

Pontypool and Blaenafon Railway
Tel: 01495 772200 or 772726

Just outside the National Park there's a different world to discover!

At Big Pit, Blaenafon, you can visit the world beneath the hills and valleys - the disappearing world of the coal miner. At this colliery, where millions of tons of prime steam coal were mined between 1880 and 1980, you can go underground to see for yourself how generations of men and horses spent their working lives. You will be provided with helmet and caplamp. An experienced miner will escort you down the 300ft shaft by cage and guide you around the underground roadways, coalface and stables. On the surface you can visit the original winding enginehouse, workshops and pithead baths, which now house exhibitions, have a meal in the miners canteen and browse in a well-stocked craft, gift and book shop. The museum is open daily from end of February to end of November, 9.30am to 5pm. Hour-long underground tours run throughout the day, with last tour beginning at 3.30pm. Ramps, toilets and special access facilities are available for disabled visitors, but prior notice is required for wheelchair-users on underground tours.

BIG PIT
PWLL MAWR
BLAENAFON Gwent NP4 9XP
Telephone: 01495-790311 • Fax: 01495-792618

Brecon

Brecon is a cathedral town of great beauty and interest, set at the confluence of the rivers Usk and Honddu. The priory church of St John was elevated to the status of cathedral in 1923, and is a fine structure dating from the 13th and 14th centuries. It was built over a Norman church that suffered during the wars for Welsh independence. The cathedral is cruciform in plan, with an early-English choir and a decorated nave. Side chapels are dedicated to various trades: tailors, weavers, tuckers, fullers and corvizors (shoemakers). Domestic buildings of the Benedictine abbey have been restored.

The parish church of St. Mary is basically a medieval building on a Norman foundation, but the tower dates from the 16th century.

In the heart of Brecon is the beautiful Calvinistic Methodist chapel, which seats a congregation of 800.

Brecon Cathedral

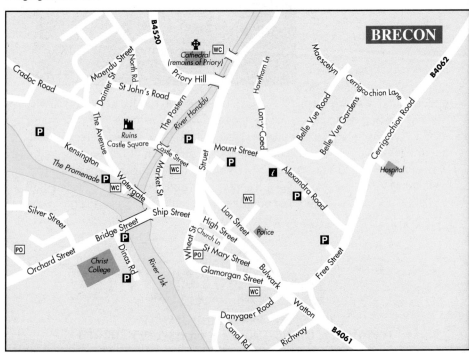

Cloaked in this breathtaking countryside and steeped in history, dating back to Norman times. Our restored Georgian Manor House offers:

Morning Coffee
Lunch
Afternoon Tea
Dinner

In a choice of both formal and informal surroundings.

Travelling in an organised group by coach?
Don't rule us out!!

Phone and invite us to quote for your requirements.
We've also got luxurious bedrooms and health club.

Peterstone Court
BRECON • WALES
TEL: 01874 665387
FAX: 01874 665376.

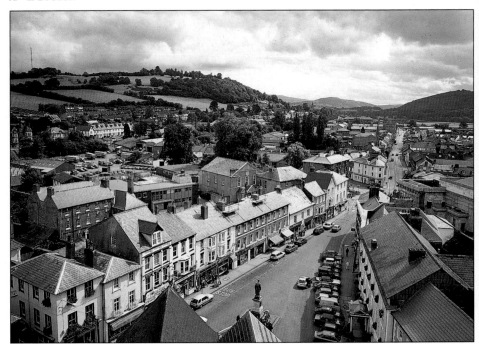

Brecon Town

The remains of Brecon Castle lie partly in the grounds of the Castle Hotel and partly in the bishop's garden. The ruins are fragments from the 12th and 13th centuries. Remains of the medieval town walls can be seen in several areas, especially along Captain's Walk which was built and used by French prisoners in the Napoleonic wars. Brecon also has some fine Georgian and Jacobean town houses.

On the other bank of the River Usk, which is spanned by an ancient bridge, is the site of Christ College. This was founded in 1542 and became a public school in 1860.

The town is the home of the South Wales Borderers - famed for their courageous defence of Rorke's Drift against the overwhelming odds in the Zulu War - and their early 19th-century barracks include a military museum. The county museum is in Glamorgan Street.

Brecon itself is a market town with a good shopping centre and excellent car parking facilities. There are ample opportunities for

sports, including a swimming pool, a tennis court, bowling greens, two golf courses - all within easy reach, and pony trekking and riding centres.

Beautiful countryside surrounds Brecon, and the Brecon Beacons are virtually on the doorstep, rising nearly 3,000 ft to provide a dramatic backdrop.

ATTRACTIONS & PLACES OF INTEREST

Brecknock Museum
The museum has a fine collection of lovespoons, together with a permanent display of rural life, archaeology and natural history of Brecknock. For further information telephone 01874 624121.

The South Wales Borderers and Monmouthshire Regiment Museum
The museum spans 280 years of military history and houses a large Zulu War display featuring the heroic defence of Rorke's Drift. Exhibits include armoury, medals, uniforms and paintings. For further information telephone 01874 623111.

Welsh Whisky
Located at Brecon's Parc Mentor, the distillery has a superb new Visitor Centre - opened by the Secretary of State for Wales on 7th May 1993 - where you can see how Welsh Whisky is made..

Whisky (or chwisgi) started life way back in 356 AD, created by a man known as Reaullt Hir of Bardsey Island, off the tip of the north Wales coast. A process of distillation had been brought to the shores of Wales by early Greek merchants. Reaullt of Bardsey adapted the process to distil 'Bragget' (sweet ale) that the monks brewed on the island, and it was the monks who went on to develop the art of distilling to produce what we now know as whisky.

The making of whisky spread throughout the Celts of the great Isles of Britain as a pain killer and medication for those wounded in battle. It

was also considered a great aphrodisiac and was called 'Uisce Beatha' ('water of life') by Celts of Ireland and the Western Isles of Scotland.

After the dissolution of the monasteries by Henry VIII, distillation was carried on by farmers using excess grain from their harvests, and this flourished among the crofters of Scotland.

The commercialisation of whisky started in Ireland in the early 17th century and then spread to Scotland. The first commercial distillery in Wales was founded by the Evan Williams family of Dale in Pembrokeshire in the early 18th century, and in the middle of the century the Daniels family of Cardigan also went into production. Both these families later emigrated to the USA to found distilleries in Kentucky and Tennessee.

More than a hundred years passed by before a major distillery was built in Wales, at Bala in 1880 by Robert Willis and Mr Price of Rhiwlas. With an issued share capital of £100,000, the distillery - sited at Frongoch, Bala - was very substantial, even by today's standards. The company closed down in 1906 in the wake of a fierce temperance movement at the turn of the century which swept Wales almost dry . As the last cask was filled in that depressed year, it was thought Welsh whisky would be lost for ever.

But in a small cellar at Brecon in 1974, Dafydd Gittins and Mal Morgan began blending Swn Y Môr Welsh Chwisgi. In 1975 the enterprise moved to a small brew house behind the Camden Arms Hotel in Brecon. Dafydd and his wife Gillian formed Brecon Brewery and the birth of Swn Y Môr Welsh whisky had begun. It took Dafydd a further six years to perfect the recipe and blend, keeping as close as possible to the original Welsh whiskies. Using herbs to filter the whisky, Dafydd unlocked the secret the world had almost forgotten.

Having rediscovered Reaullt Hir's secret Dafydd and Gillian expanded to new premises on Brecon's Ffwdgrech Estate in 1982. In 1984 they added a liqueur, then a gin, then vodka, and in 1986 they introduced a single malt whisky called Prince of Wales. Thus the spirits of Wales were born.

In August 1991 the company moved to the new distillery at Brecon's Parc Menter, which will be fully operational by the summer of 1995. For further information telephone 01874 622926.

Guildhall Theatre, Brecon
Tel: 01874 623069
Coliseum Film Centre, Brecon
Tel: 01874 622501
Jazz Aberhonddu
Brecon Jazz Festival

To use the words of George Melly: "Brecon means jazz, means happiness, means golden weekends."

The history of this modest Mid Wales market town (from which Davy Gam Esquire set forth to fight for his king at Agincourt, and whose regiment defied the Zulus at Rorke's Drift) provides no clue to its development in the 1980s as home to one of the world's most respected and irresistible celebrations of jazz.

When the festival began in 1984 it was a community initiative inspired by a visit to the Breda Jazz Festival in Holland. It is still run largely by the community (with over 300 volunteers involved during festival weekend), but its reputation is international and its audience drawn from all corners of Britain and beyond. Its

Brecon Jazz Festival

appeal is two-fold: to the jazz enthusiast for its glorious world class music, and to the casual visitor for the atmosphere, the open air bandstands and spectacular setting.

In some extraordinary way, the tranquil town beneath the Beacons has absorbed and withstood the onslaught of the tens of thousands of pilgrims who create, for one annual August weekend, what is described in the national press as "an atmosphere of collective exuberance" and "an overwhelming sense of occasion."

Improvisation is one of the essential ingredients of jazz. It is also an ingredient in the success of Brecon's festival. With no large concert hall or theatre, Brecon has welcomed some of the jazz world's most legendary figures to its market hall, its town hall, its school and its open-air car parks. American superstars mingle with young Welsh aspirants, and the quality of the programming draws participants back year after year to experience again the particular charm of Brecon Jazz.

Bronllys

The local church has a detached tower. In times of trouble women and children were sent to the upper floor, while the cattle were kept safely in the lower part. The nearby 12th-century Bronllys Castle is one and a half miles south on the A479 Talgarth to Bronllys road.

Bwlch

A small village affording beautiful views as the A40 climbs up to it from Abergavenny to Brecon, Bwlch lies four miles south-east of Llangorse Lake and is within the national park. Further views of the Brecon Beacons open up to the south, beyond the village. To the north west of Bwlch are remains of Blaen Llyaft Castle.

The New Inn
Bwlch
Tel: (01874) 730215
Bed & Breakfast
Twin-Bedded Rooms
En Suite Facility
Full English Breakfast
Good Food & Real Ales Bar menu always available Children's meals Guest Beers.

Caerleon

The town of Caerleon lies four miles up the Usk from Newport and is one of the most historic in Wales, boasting strong associations with the Romans and King Arthur. The town was one of the three foremost legionary bases in Britain, the others being Chester and York. The fort covered five and a half acres, and the outline of the ramparts can be clearly traced on the west and south-west sides, although houses still cover the rest of the site. The parish church stands on the foundations of the old basilica, and a large section of the wall and the legionary barracks can be seen in the Prysg field. The showpiece, however, is the Roman amphitheatre, excavated by Sir Mortimer Wheeler in 1920. In the Middle Ages, it was covered with grass and known as King Arthur's Round Table. That powerful romancer, Geoffrey of Monmouth, cast Caerleon in the role of King Arthur's Camelot and Tennyson, the poet, came here to capture the Arthurian atmosphere when he was writing the 'Idylls of the King'. More recent excavations have exposed the remains of the Roman Baths, which are interpreted in a new exhibition centre at the site.

ATTRACTIONS & PLACES OF INTEREST

Caerleon Legionary Museum
Tel: 01633 423134

Caerleon Roman Amphitheatre
Tel: 01633 421656

Caerleon Roman Fortress Baths
Tel: 01633 422518

Capel-y-Ffin

Small hamlet near the head of the Llanthony valley, in the Black Mountains. A neo-Benedictine community was founded here in 1869 and they built the monastery and a church named Llanthony Abbey. The picturesque little white church, now in ruins, with the drunken bell-turret, is worth a visit.

Castell Dinas

Located off the A479 Talgarth-Crickhowell road (1,476 ft) is the second highest hill fort of the park, exceeded only by Crug Hywel. Of Iron Age origin, it was refortified in Norman and medieval times.

Craig-y-Nos

A former palatial home of the Victorian prima donna Adelina Patti, located off the A4067 in the Tawe valley 4½ miles north of Ystradgynlais. The house is not open to the public, but 40 acres of grounds which were acquired as a country park by the national park in 1976, offer pleasant walks through woodlands and meadows.

Crickhowell

The town nestles beneath Pen Cerrig-Calch (2,302ft) mountain. This pleasant little town, on the main road between Abergavenny and

Crickhowell Bridge

Brecon, is happily placed in one of the most beautiful sections of the valley of the Usk. The river winds through rich parklands to flow under the old, thirteen-arched bridge which is the chief architectural glory of Crickhowell.

Strongly buttressed and spanning the River Usk, the bridge was built in the 17th century. It displays segmented arches with double-arch rings built in two orders, with the stones forming the outer ring smaller than those in the inner ring. Two of the arches have been rebuilt. The bridge has been widened on the upstream side, and the total span is 140 yards.

Only the motte and bailey, parts of the wall, and a small round tower remain of Crickhowell Castle, which was built towards the end of the 11th century. Owain Glyndwr stormed and destroyed most of the castle in 1403.

Some three quarters of a mile west of the town is Gwern Vale House, where Sir George Everest was born in 1790. Mount Everest was

Waterfall, Nr Llyn-y-Fan Fawr

named after this great military engineer, who did much of his surveying in India. He is buried in the churchyard at Crickhowell. Also west of the town is the 14th century gatehouse at Porthmawr, which has survived a now-vanished Tudor mansion that belonged to the Herbert family. The Craig-y-Cilau nature reserve lies two miles south-west of the town. The Welsh Brigade Museum is close to Crickhowell at Cwrt-y-Gollen Camp.

The Monmouthshire and Brecon Canal runs along the foot of the hills: one of the most delightful holiday waterways in the whole of Britain and navigable from Pontypool to Brecon itself. It offers an unrivalled series of locks, towpaths, tunnels and swing bridges in splendid scenery all the way along the Usk valley.

Narrow roads twist northwards from Crickhowell into the slender valley of the Grwyne Fechan, which curves around the back of the Sugar Loaf. Here is the little village of Llanbedr Ystrad Yw, with its ancient church and air of complete peace. The Grwyne Fechan is a walking and riding region, for it is a dead end for motorists. The Grwyne Fawr and the smaller stream join at Llanbedr: again a valley with no drivable road out of it at the top end, which is guarded by a small reservoir. The two Grwyne valleys show the Black Mountains at their best, and the Grwyne Fawr has the tiny church of Partrishow, with its early Tudor rood screen, decorated with Welsh dragons, wall murals with the figure of Death, and an oaken roof. There are beautiful views from the churchyard.

ATTRACTIONS & PLACES OF INTEREST

Crickhowell Castle
Site open to visitors.

Cwmyoy

Hamlet in the Black Mountains' Vale of Ewyas, some 4 miles south of Llanthony. It is noted for its 'crookedest church in Wales', with is tower and nave which are askew.

Dan-yr-Ogof Showcaves
Located in the Tawe valley, almost next-door to Craig-y-Nos, the site is claimed to be the largest public show-cave complex in Western Europe. It is one of the most popular tourist attractions in the park. There are guided tours through the system with its stalactite and stalagmite formations, which include access to the vast Cathedral Cave, where there are models of Stone Age man.

Defynnog

The village church with its 15th-century tower, was formerly the centre of a large parish, houses a 12th-century font bearing the only Runic inscription in Wales. The village lies nine miles west of Brecon and was in the the 19th-century important for it's cattle and sheep markets.

Grosmont

An old-world village set on a hillside, Grosmont stands amid beautiful scenery by the River Monnow on the border between Gwent, Hereford and Worcester. The single street of the village runs between the castle and the church. Grosmont is small by today's standards and is an important centre for anglers. The church of St Nicholas carries a massive octagonal tower topped by a spire, and has a large unfinished nave arcade. Inside there is a huge flat-faced stone knight which is thought to be an effigy of one of

Edmund Grouchback's descendants.

Grosmont Castle was one of three castles erected in the vicinity by the Norman Lords of Abergavenny to protect the Welsh/English border; the others are Skenfrith and White Castle. It is believed that the castle at Grosmont dates back to 1163. The structure was largely rebuilt during the reign of Henry III, who stayed here for a time until Llywelyn the Great stormed the building and forced Henry and his queen to escape at night. In 1410 Owain Glyndwr burned the town and seized the castle, establishing Rhys Gethin here to hold the position. English reinforcements were hurriedly sent under the command of Harry Monmouth (later to be Henry V),and the Welsh were completely routed. The castle is now under the care of Cadw (Welsh Historic Monuments), and little remains of it except the inner ward gateway, the keep, the containing wall with two drum towers, and a 13th-century octagonal chimney which once served the banqueting hall.

Libanus

Situated on the A470 south-west of Brecon. From the hamlet there is access to the Brecon Beacons Mountain Centre.Close to the village is the National Trust's Blaenglyn Farm (contact the National Trust for opening hours).

Llanddeusant

Located in the foothills of the Black Mountain, this hamlet is a popular starting point for a visit to the lake of Llyn y Fan Fach, source of the Sawdde river.

Llanddew

A hamlet three miles north-east of Brecon. Apart from the unusual cruciform church, Llanddew's main claim to fame is the remarkable site of the former Bishop's Palace in which Archdeacon of Brecon - better known as Giraldus Cambrensis, or Gerald of Wales - resided for twenty-five years and wrote his well-known 'Itinerary through Wales'. Only a few ruined walls of the palace remain today.

Llandeilo

(See page 30)

Llandovery

(See page 31)

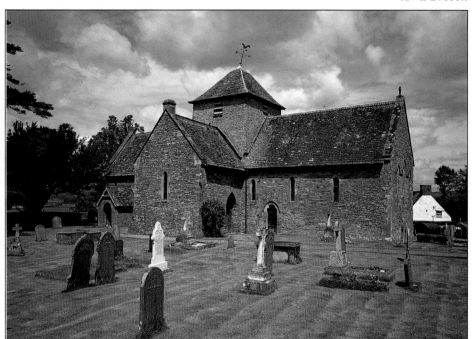

Llanddew Church

Llanelieu

This village lies some 2 miles east of Talgarth. Llanelieu has a remote little Anglican church with a 14th century rood-screen and in the porch are 7th and 9th-century pillar stones. The other fame to the village is Llanelieu Court, which is said to have originated as a 14th century monastic cell of Llanthony Priory.

Llanfilo

This hamlet is situated about two miles west of Talgarth. The little church, among the most attractive in the area, features lovely oak pews, altar rails and pulpit dating from the 17th century, and rood-loft and screen from c1500. The porch and timbered roof date from 1350 and the font is pre-Norman.

Llangorse Lake & Village

Llangorse Lake (Llyn Syfaddan) lies five miles south-east of Brecon and is the largest natural lake in South Wales, and the second largest in the country. Although this shallow lake, with its low, marshy, reeded banks is not visually spectacular, it lies in a very attractive setting with hills and mountains on three sides. The lake is about two miles long by half a mile wide with a shoreline of nearly four miles. On its east side the west flanks of the Black Mountains rise steeply, with the conical summit of Mynydd Troed (1,997ft) and the flat-topped Mynydd Llangorse (1,661ft). To the south-east the slopes of Mynydd Llangorse drop down to the 650 ft high pass at Bwlch, which leads to the Usk Valley. Buckland Hill rises to 1,038 ft west of Bwlch, and is half hidden by Allt yr Esgair (1,250ft) - the wooded hill south of the lake. To

Llangorse Lake

the west and north-west the hills are lower, but the scene to the south-west is dominated by the Brecon Beacons, with the high ridge from Craig Pwllfa (2,504 ft) leading west to Cribin (2,608 ft) and the main summits of Pen-y-fan (2,906 ft) and Corn-du (2,863 ft).

Llangorse is a pleasant village situated close by the lake and has a 14th century church with a small tower. Although heavily restored in the last century, the building retains a good 15th century wagon roof, a wide south aisle with an arcade of four bays, and an ancient inscribed stone. To the west is Llanfihangel Tal-y-llyn, and a road leads to the shore. The small church here carries a medieval tower and was restored in 1870. On the south shore almost opposite Llangorse is the church and scattered hamlet of Llangasty Talyllyn. The church, situated right on the water's edge, was built in 1849 for a relative of Robert Raikes, the pioneer of Sunday schools in the late 18th century. It has many interesting modern interior details, and the tower offers a good viewpoint. To the south west is Treberfedd, a mansion built in a Tudor style for the Raikes family, descendants of Robert.

Llangynidr

Situated halfway between Abergavenny and Brecon, this small village lies in one of the most attractive stretches of the Usk Valley. To the north of the river are 1,038 ft Buckland Hill and Myarth, with the lower slopes of 1,6612 ft Mynydd Llangorse visible between them above the village of Bwlch. On the south side are Mynydd Llangynidr and Mynydd Llangattock, both over 1,700 ft high, with the conical peak of Tor-y-Foel (1,806 ft) overlooking the Dyffryn Crawnan to the west. The B4560 from Llangynidr to Beaufort makes a winding ascent over Mynydd Llangattock, reaching a summit viewpoint of 1,694 ft. The panorama from the top includes the Usk Valley and many of the

Llangorse Lake

summits of the Black Mountains, including Mynydd Llangorse, Pen Allt-mawr, Pen Cerrig-Calch, Crug Mawr, and the Sugar Loaf.

Llangynidr has a picturesque old bridge over the River Usk, dating from c1600, which has six arches and massive cutwaters. Attractive walks along the river extend in both directions from the south side. Between the Usk and the main part of the village lies the Monmouthshire and Brecon Canal, now in use for pleasure craft. Nearly one mile east of the village, on the B4558 Crickhowell road and situated across the canal, is Aberhoyw - an attractive farmhouse with a coat of arms dated 1726. Nearby is the modern house of Worcester Lodge, situated in a fine position by the river almost opposite Gliffaes, an Italianate mansion with a beautiful garden containing rare shrubs and trees. The property now serves as a hotel.

Llananthony

This hamlet is located in the Llanthony Valley in the Black Mountains. The popular tourist attraction of Llanthony is the 12th century ruins of Llanthony Priory, founded by Norman Marcher Lord Walter de Lacy as an Augustinian monastery. The site offers good hill-walking on the Black Mountains ridges.

Llyn-y-Fan Fach & Llyn-y-Fan Fawr

These two remote lakes can only be reached on foot, either from the minor road from Trecastle to Glyntawe, or by a more arduous trudge below the Black Mountain's scarp from neighbouring Llyn y Fan Fach. Llynd y Fan Fawr is even more remote than Llyn y Fan Fach; this lake lies at the foot of the Fan Hir ridge of the Black Mountain, and at 1,950 ft is the highest in the park.

Brecon Mountain Railway

Merthyr Tydfil

Merthyr Tydfil takes its name from St Tydfil, daughter of the Lord of Brycheiniog (Brecon) who was martyred for her Christian faith by pagans in AD 480. The town is situated in the Taff Valley. It became a coalmining town and records show local iron workings here as early as the 16th century. By 1831 Merthyr Tydfil had become the largest town in Wales. In 1804 the first steam locomotive made its journey between Merthyr Tydfil and Abercynon, built by the Cornish engineer Richard Trevithick. Penydarren Works produced the first rails to be made in Wales, for the Liverpool and Manchester railway, and later made cables for the Menai Bridge.

After the First World War heavy industry moved out of the town to areas near the coast seaports, and Merthyr Tydfil was left in a desperate situation with half the population unemployed. The community is now supported by light industries. Cyfarthfa Castle was built in 1825 and now serves the town as a museum and art gallery. The parish church of St. Tydfil, of 14th-century origin, has undergone a great deal of alteration. It contains three inscribed stones, one of which dates from around the 9th century. An iron bridge over the Taff is believed to be the oldest in existence. The composer, Dr Joseph

Parry was born in Merthyr Tydfil in 1814, and Kier Hardie, the pioneer of socialism, was the town's MP during the early years of the 20th century. To the north of the town is the Brecon Beacons National Park and the Penmoelallt Forest nature reserve.

ATTRACTIONS & PLACES OF INTEREST

Brecon Mountain Railway
Pant. Tel: 01685 4854
Cyfarthfa Castle Museum
Tel: 01685 723112
Joseph Parry's Cottage
4 Chapel Row. Tel: 01685 73117
Ynysfach Engine House
Tel: 01685 721858

Garwnant Forest Visitor Centre
Situated off the A470, 5 miles north-west of Merthyr Tydfil.

Victoria Festival Park

This beautiful landscaped park, of more than 63 acres, boasting hillside woodlands and wetlands, lakes and formal gardens, is unique to the area. It still has many Garden Festival features of 1992, but also includes beautiful country walks, public works of art, gardens and special environmental centres to make an enjoyable and interesting visit for young and old alike.

Festival Park has its own Visitor Centre (and café) where you can discover more about the 'Iron Barons', the industrial boom of the 19th century, the thrills and excitement of Garden Festival Wales, and the subsequent plans for the future of the new Victoria village development.

The gardens include many interesting features. For example, tucked up in the hillside overlooking the park is an exceptional opportunity to explore the hidden depths of pondlife at the wetlands. In addition, in the woodlands, visitors can experience how man can

Horticultural excellence and captivating country trails.

Festival Park has retained the best landscape features of the 1992 Garden Festival Wales. The Visitor and Education Centres highlight the industrial history and future development of this scenic valley location.

The exotic Tropical Planthouse and Ornamental Gardens, the Woodland and Wetland Centres, the Lake, Oriental Pavilion and sculpture collection provide an oasis of peace and tranquillity. Youngsters can enjoy the Children's Playground, the Treehouse, Bird's Nest and Snake Maze and climb the 'Stairway to the Stars'. There is free car and coach parking alongside a souvenir shop and cafe. Festival Park has world-wide appeal and is accessible to the disabled.

A 'Warm Welsh Welcome' awaits! Open all year. Free admission.

2 miles south of Ebbw Vale on A4046 (Newport road). Signposted from A465(T)
(Heads of the Valleys road). 17 miles north of M4 (Junction 28), follow A467 to
A4046 (Ebbw Vale road).

For information on our Varied Events programme,
please telephone 01495 350010,
or write to, The Manager, Festival Park, Visitor Centre,
Victoria Road, Ebbw Vale, Gwent NP3 6UF

Festival Park

live in harmony with the environment. Enjoy the Tree House, a man-sized bird's nest, a snake maze and a willow dome.

Not everything at Festival Park is orientated towards the British way of life. The park includes an Oriental Pavilion which has been built to demonstrate the characteristics of Far Eastern architecture. A tropical planthouse contains many exotic and carnivorous plants from Malaysia and Singapore, as well as cacti, succulents and Mediterranean plants.

There is plenty for the family to explore at the exciting Festival Park, which is open all year round, seven days a week, between dawn and dusk. Admission is free. For further information, and up-to-date details of a full Events Programme, telephone 01495 350010.

Monmouth

Monmouth is a market town and has many Tudor and Georgian buildings in a network of old streets. Three rivers flow round the town: the Trothy, Monnow and Wye. The town is sited where the River Monnow flows into the Wye, an important strategic position from which the whole of South Wales could be controlled. The Romans had a base near Monmouth, an important link in the chain of roads that ran one way through Caerwent and Caerleon, and another way to Wrexham, Caersws, and Chester. The Normans made the town a springboard for their penetration of South Wales. The first lords of Monmouth were Bretons.

Monnow Bridge, situated in the town centre, is the only Norman fortified bridge to survive in Britain. The fortified tower is on the bridge itself and was built in 1260 as one of the four medieval gates into the town. The bridge has three semi-circular arches with a total span of 38 yards and each arch has three wide ribs. The bridge was originally constructed for pedestrians and horses only. More than anywhere else in the borderlands area known as the Welsh Marches, Monmouthshire has remained mostly Welsh in the use of language and place-names. In fact, Wales has now recovered one of its lost provinces, as the county is once more known by its title of Gwent.

The original castle here was probably a simple wooden structure on a motte, but no definite trace of either remains. Monmouth was listed in the Domesday Book of 1086 as part of Herefordshire, and was the headquarters of the Marcher Lordship of Monmouth. Henry Somerset, son of the second Marquis of Worcester, built Great Castle House on the site of the old castle's Round Tower in 1673. By 1801 the house had become a girls' school, and in 1875 it started its career as the headquarters of the Royal Monmouthshire Engineer Militia. Restoration of the castle's medieval remains which peacefully rise above the River Monnow was begun by the government in 1913, and both castle and house are open to visitors. The former castle was the birthplace of Henry V.

Shire Hall is situated in Agincourt Square and was built in 1724 on the site of an Elizabethan Market Hall. Until 1939 the Assizes were held here, and in 1839 John Frost and the Chartist leaders were tried here for high treason after the Newport riots. A statue of Henry V was placed in a recess of the wall of the Shire Hall in 1792. Alongside this statue is one of Charles S Rolls, founder of Rolls Royce and a pioneer airman, who was the first person to fly the English Channel

both ways without landing. Monmouth's Nelson Museum contains a comprehensive collection of material associated with Lord Nelson - including sextants, Nelson's fighting sword, and models of his ships. To the east of the town a wooded hill known as Kymin (840 ft) is surmounted by an 18th-century Round House and Naval Temple. The temple was visited by Nelson in 1802 and commemorates a galaxy of admirals unequalled by any other age or country. Excellent views over the Monnow and Wye valleys are afforded by Kymin. The site is run by the National Trust.

The parish church of St Mary retains a decorated-style tower and spire, but the rest of the church was the work of GE Street in 1881, who replaced a Georgian church built by Francis Smith of Warwick. The church of St Thomas has a fine Norman chancel arch, an original north door, and a 19th-century pseudo-Norman porch. The interesting font and galleries were made from timber supplied by the Duke of Beaufort. The part of the town where St Thomas's Church is sited is known as Overmonnow, and was once a centre for cap-making. The close-fitting caps from here were the 'Monmouth Caps' mentioned in Shakespeare's Henry V. The River Monnow has coarse fish and trout and attracts many keen anglers. Monmouth Agricultural Show is held annually at the end of August.

St Peter's Church at Dixton, near Monmouth, is on a site that was an ancient place of worship. This church has been subject to severe flooding, and brass plates on the north side of the chancel arch record heights of three high floods.

ATTRACTIONS & PLACES OF INTEREST

Monmouth Castle
For details contact the local Tourist Information Centre.

Monmouth Museum
Tel: 0600 3519

THE TAFF TRAIL
for walkers and cyclists

FOR ALL THE FAMILY

The Taff Trail is a mainly off-road cyclepath and footpath that links Wales' Capital City Cardiff with Brecon, a market town set in the heart of the Brecon Beacons National Park. Largely traffic-free the 55 mile Trail passes through a variety of landscapes and there are many sites of interest and industrial heritage either adjacent or close. Most of the route follows easy gradients with the occasional steeper section and is suitable for all ages and abilities.

FOLLOW THE TRAIL

The official start of the Trail is on the waterfront at Cardiff Bay. It is marked by a bronze celtic ring sculpture. Leaving the city the Trail passes through the narrow Taff Gorge guarded by Castell Coch, a splendid Victorian Castle. The Trail follows the Taff Valley Northwards to Merthyr using a network of disused canal banks, tramroads and railroads. From Merthyr the character of the Trail changes as it leaves the valley behind and enters the Brecon Beacons. The walker can either follow a series of footpaths up the Taf Fawr Valley and onto Brecon, or continue to follow the cycle route up the Eastern Taf Fechan valley. This uses a combination of forestry tracks, old railway lines and country lanes. The final part of the route takes the traveller along the peaceful Usk Valley to end in Brecon.

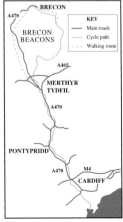

FOR FURTHER INFORMATION

Information on the Trail including a complimentary set of postcards are available on receipt of a 60p stamped addressed envelope from:

TAFF TRAIL PROJECT, C/O GROUNDWORK MERTHYR & CYNON, FEDW HIR, LLWYDCOED, ABERDARE CF44 0DX • TEL: 01685 883880
Please quote reference number: BBG/95

69

Myddfai

This village is reached by any of numerous lanes from Llandovery and is associated with Llyn y Fan Fach's 'Lady of the Lake' legend. A memorial to the legend and the 'Physicians of Myddfai' can be found in the church porch.

Offa's Dyke Path

This long-distance footpath of 168 miles runs from Prestatyn on the North Wales coast to the Severn estuary near Chepstow. The path was opened in 1971.

Partrishow

The small hamlet of Partrishow can be found in the quiet lanes and hills above Abergavenny. The pretty and tiny church of Partrishow contains an exceptional rood screen, one of the finest in Wales. The delicate, very elaborate screen, carved in oak, was the work of highly skilled Tudor craftsmen. The isolated church evokes a strong sense of times past. It dates from the 11th century and features a Norman font and macabre wall painting of a skeleton depicting death.

A cul-de-sac road from the church to the north leads through the forested slopes of the remote Grwyne Fawr valley.

Pontypool

This industrial town was the centre of a predominantly coalmining and tinplate district and in 1720 became the first town in Britain to successfully produce tinplate. About two miles east is Llandegfedd Reservoir, which supplies water to Cardiff and offers sailing and fishing. The Monmouthshire and Brecon Canal runs for thirty-three and a half miles from Pontypool to Brecon.

ATTRACTIONS & PLACES OF INTEREST

Pontypool Ski Slope
Tel: 01495 756955

The Valley Inheritance
Tel: 01495 752036 or 752043

Raglan

Raglan Castle was erected on the site of an 11th or 12-century motte and bailey structure. The present building dates from 1430 to the early 17th century and the Great Yellow Tower of Gwent is one of its oldest parts. The parish church has a pinnacled tower and contains a few mutilated effigies of the Somersets, damaged during the siege of the castle by Cromwell's troops. The castle is open to the public and is run by Cadw. One of the two interesting windows displays various coats of arms. Three miles west is the fine Regency mansion of Clytha House, about four and a half miles west-north-west is the notable early 18th-century Pant-y-Gotre bridge over the River Usk.

ATTRACTIONS & PLACES OF INTEREST

Raglan Castle
Tel: 01291 690228

Sennybridge

Situated where the Afon Senni flows into the River Usk about eight miles west of Brecon, Sennybridge lies on the north edge of the Brecon Beacons National Park. It is an important centre for the marketing of sheep and cattle for the surrounding area. Castell Du, now a ruin, stands

on the west bank of the Senni and is believed to have been constructed during the 13th century. It comprises a small round keep with a smaller building attached, and at one time was used as a prison by the keepers of Fforest Fawr.

ATTRACTIONS & PLACES OF INTEREST

Glynderi Pottery

If you take the turning at Sennybridge towards Pentrefelin, just after crossing the Llwyncyntefin Bridge over the River Usk you will discover Glynderi Pottery within the coachhouse of this 17th century Welsh longhouse.

Ruth Lyle makes beautiful stoneware pots here. Attractive ranges of domestic wares are displayed in the large gallery alongside one-off pots, bells, frog mugs and hand-modelled little animals. There are also carefully selected gifts, such as jewellery, Welsh lovespoons, hand-blown glass, wooden carvings and batik clothes.

Visitors are welcome to browse and watch

Storey Arms

any work in progress, such as preparing clay, throwing and glazing. Children are encouraged to model clay in a free activity area set aside for them. The pottery is open all year and there are picnic tables in a lovely garden. For further information telephone 01874 636564.

Skenfrith

Situated close to the English border about eight miles north-west of Monmouth, this village stands beside the River Monnow. The river is excellent for trout fishing. Skenfrith's 13th-century castle is one of three forming a triangle of defence, the others being Grosmont and White Castle. Ruins include a round tower enclosed by a four-sided curtain wall and a moat. The wall probably had five towers, but only four remain. It ceased to be of importance after the end of the Welsh uprisings, and was probably in ruins by the 16th century. The castle is now owned by the National Trust. The local church also dates back to the 13th century and has an impressive, partially-timbered tower.

Storey Arms

Storey Arms lies in the heart of the Brecon Beacons National Park. It is at the top of a 439m (1440 ft) pass through the mountains and close to the highest peaks in South Wales. Pont ar Daf at Storey Arms is the place from where most people set off to walk to the Beacons' distinctive, flat-topped summit of Pen y Fan (2,907 ft). There are a number of different paths to the summit, and it is advisable to make reference to an Ordnance Survey map to get away from the main paths which become very busy during the spring and summer seasons.

There is a car park and Outside Education Centre at the site. Storey Arms is also a Mountain Rescue Post.

Talgarth

This small market town is set at the foot of the Black Mountains. Talgarth lies in the Brecon Beacons National Park and to the south-east rise the lofty peaks of Waun Fach (2,660 ft) and Pen-y-Gader (2,624 ft). Eight cattle markets were once held here annually. The church is dedicated to St Gwendoline and dates from the 13th century. It was restored in 1873. The south aisle displays an excellent 14th century sepulchral slab. A square 14th century pele tower standing at the east end of a local bridge was once used as a lookout post, but has since been converted into a house.

Hywel Harris, a founder of Methodism in Wales, came from the village. He intended to enter the Church of England, but after he was refused ordination on three occasions he became a wandering preacher. Later in life he set up a communal farming centre at nearby Trefeca, where the inhabitants lived an almost monastic life. He was supported in this venture by the Countess of Huntingdon. After his death in 1773 and subsequent burial in Talgarth churchyard, a chapel was erected at Trefeca to his memory.

ATTRACTIONS & PLACES OF INTEREST

Bronllys Castle
For more details contact the local Tourist Information Centre.

Hywel Harris Museum
Tel: 01874 711423

Talybont

This village is situated on the Monmouthshire-Brecon canal in the Usk valley. The town provides a good centre for exploring the canal, either on the towpath or by

Talybont Falls

boat. The large Talybont Reservoir is a couple of miles to the south. The reservoir is one of many reservoirs set in the Brecon Beacons and built to serve industrial South Wales. This particular one takes its name from Talybont-on-Usk - which lies to the north - and serves the town of Newport. It is situated in a wooded valley and provides a wonderful refuge for wild fowl.

Taff Trail
See page 69

Trecastle

This village is situated on the A40, about 10 miles west of Brecon and was once a notable stage on the Gloucester-Llandovery mail and stage-coach route, where horses were changed. In Norman times the lord of Brecon had an outpost here: the remaining tree-clad motte and bailey castle is the largest in the national park,

Talybont Forest

CASTLE COACHING INN

Trecastle, Brecon, Powys, LD3 8UH
Telephone: 01874 636354 · Fax: 01874 636457

The Castle Coaching Inn was once a coaching inn on the main route between London and Fishguard. It is situated in the small village of Trecastle, midway between Brecon and Llandovery, in the heart of the Brecon Beacons.

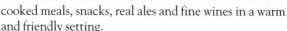

The Bar and Dining Room with open fires offer first class home cooked meals, snacks, real ales and fine wines in a warm and friendly setting.

All ten bedrooms are good sized, with private bathrooms, central heating, colour TV, clock radio, tea/coffee making facilities and telephone.

but only the mound and other earthworks are to be seen today.

Trefeca

This hamlet is about one mile south west of Talgarth and is noted for its Trefeca College theological study centre. This is the site of the community set up by Howell Harris in 1752 and the residence he erected is still occupied by the college, together with modern additions. On the outskirts of the village there is the 16th-century College Farm where in 1768 Harris's supporter, the Countess of Huntingdon, established an academy for Methodist preachers.

Tretower

A small village situated on the A429 about two and a half miles north of Crickhowell.

Lying beside the Rhiangoll stream are the remains of a 13th-century Norman castle and a fortified mansion of the 14th and 15th centuries. The land was granted to the Norman knight Picard by the Lord of Brecon, and he constructed a motte surrounded by a polygonal stone wall. After the Welsh had managed to capture it for a short while in 1233, the English strengthened it by building a tall circular keep inside the wall. To this they added three round towers. It was later rebuilt and turned into one of the finest early fortified mansions in Wales. It is built round a courtyard and has an impressive gatehouse. After 1777 the Court became a farmhouse and by 1936 had fallen into disrepair. Through the efforts of Colonel Sir John Lloyd and the Brecknock Society it was preserved, and latterly the Department of the Environment have taken over and carried out extensive repairs to restore it to its former glory. Both castle and court are open to the public. The main room is a large 15th century banqueting hall, and overlooking the courtyard is

Tretower Castle

a gallery dating from the 14th century. The mystical poet Henry Vaughan lived here during the 17th century.

Usk Castle
For more details contact the local Tourist Information Centre.

Tretower Court & Castle
Open all year. Tel: 01874 730279

Gwent Ski Centre
Llanllywel. Tel: 012913 2652

Usk

This old market town is situated on the river of the same name. Overlooking Usk are the ruins of a castle which was founded by the de Clare family as a Marcher lord's stronghold in the 12th century. The de Clares built a small square keep with earthworks; then in the 13th century the outer bailey and gatehouse were added, and later that century the large round tower was constructed. During the 15th century, other buildings were added to the outer ward. The castle supported the royalists during the civil war and was subsequently dismantled.

Beneath the town are the remains of an old Roman settlement called Burrium. The church of St Mary's was once attached to a Benedictine priory of nuns and dates back to the 13th century. Inside there is a notable Tudor screen, which was restored in 1899, and a 17th-century pulpit. The nave is of decorated style, and the porches perpendicular. A 13th-century gabled priory gateway stands near the churchyard. Cefntilla Court, built in 1616 and restored in 1856, lies two and a half miles north-east of Usk and contains fine pictures and pieces of porcelain. The town is a good touring centre: Brecon Beacons National Park lies north-west, and to the east above Chepstow is the Wye Valley. Raglan Castle stands five miles north-east.

ATTRACTIONS & PLACES OF INTEREST

Gwent Rural Life Museum
Tel: 012913 3777

Ystradfelte

This hamlet in the upper Mellte valley is located on the border of the Brecon Beacons National Park. The landscape is very different here from the other areas of the park, with wooded gauges, waterfalls, caves and potholes instead of open mountainside. The geology of the rocks changes here from limestone to old red sandstone, from which the main bulk of the Beacons are formed.

Ystradgynlais

Ystradgynlais is a Tawe valley town lying on the border of the Brecon Beacons to the north and the industrial towns to the south. A little to the south-west is the well-preserved mansion of Ynyscedwyn, which has been converted into a watch factory. The parish church of St Mary's dates from 1648. Farther up the valley are fine examples of limestone scenery. On the other side of the valley the Ffynnon Ddu (Black Spring) water gushes forth from a gloomy cavern.

Talybont Reservoir

Welcome to the Heart of Wales

The serene and beautiful countryside of Radnorshire is a great adventure playground for visitors of all ages. Pony trekking, mountain biking, birdwatching and paragliding are favourite pastimes, while there are wonderful opportunities to enjoy stunning vistas and to seek out ancient churches, historic sites and nature and sculpture trails. Even motoring is still a pleasure here. Narrow roads and lanes lead you off the beaten track to hidden, secret places, far from the madding crowd.

Along with a refreshingly unhurried pace of life, discover too the many charms of Radnorshire's delightful old towns. Llandrindod Wells, a Victorian spa town famous for its August Victorian Festival, is a popular retreat for fishermen and golfers. The 5th century market town of Rhayader is the gateway to the magnificent elan Valley, and eventful Presteigne has deservedly earned the title "The Town of Festivals". Then there is the border town of Knighton, with the best-preserved section of Offa's Dyke and a Heritage Centre dedicated to its history.

Despite its out-of-the-way attraction, Radnorshire is very accessible. Served by the Shrewsbury-Swansea Heart of Wales rail route, it is also only 3 hours from London and even less from Birmingham and Manchester. And with a wide choice of accommodation, award-winning restaurants and welcoming pubs, here awaits the promise of a true taste of the real Wales.

Llyn Clywedog

Along the Heart of Wales Railway

Leaving medieval Shrewsbury and the high hills of the Long Mynd, the Heart of Wales railway runs 120 mile beyond the green, rolling hills of the borderlands to the higher, tree-clad slopes of Radnor and the Brecon Beacons, where the buzzard and the red kite wheel in the skies above.

Slipping away to the west at Craven Arms, the train heads towards central Wales along its single-track lifeline.

The train stops at Knighton, the mid point of the Offa's Dyke earthworks, an 8th century fortification 175 miles long, defining the border between England and Wales. Knighton is the home of both the Offa's Dyke Centre and the Offa's Dyke Association. As with many of the towns and villages from here on, much of Knighton's charm and interest derives from its refusal to bow to the demands of fashionable development, and it retains many of the characteristics of a traditional market town.

As the train single carriage rolls away from Knighton, it passes the hills, forests, rivers and ubiquitous sheep which characterise this landscape; over the thirteen arches of Knucklas viaduct; through Dolau ("Dolly" to the locals and one of the prettiest stations along the line); and on to Llandrindod Wells, the largest and most famous of the Victorian spa towns. It was to the wells of Llandrindod, Builth, Llangammarch and Llanwrtyd that this railway line brought visitors from the conurbations in their thousands during the Victorian and Edwardian eras. Here they sought cures for a variety of ailments via the magical properties of the saline, sulphurous or barium chloride waters. With this boom came an explosion of building in the guise of hotels, pavilions, shopping emporia and villas and much of the architecture from the 1860s to the 1930s remains intact and little altered.

Llandrindod, spacious and unhurried and noted for its bowling facilities, celebrates its Victorian heyday each August. You will find a walk along the tree-lined avenue to the town's lake, or to the spa exhibition and open air cafeteria in Rock Park, both bracing and rewarding.

From here the train heads for Builth on the River Wye, home of the Royal Welsh Show, the Wyeside Arts Centre, regular collectors' fairs and a huge array of sporting facilities.

Then on through Cilmeri, the resting place of the last native Prince of Wales - killed by the English in 1282 - and onto Llangammarch at the foot of the Eppynt hills to Llanwrtyd, the smallest town in Britain. Llanwrtyd has a red kite centre, and annual events and competitions devoted to beer drinking, a man-versus-horse-versus-bike race, and bog snorkelling! Surrounded by glorious countryside, Llanwrtyd is an excellent centre for walking and mountain biking.

From Llanwrtyd the train moves on to its next link along the line - Llandovery, a bustling market town and tourist centre, described by George Borrow in 1854 "the pleasantest little town in which I have halted in the course of my wanderings." Influenced by New Age travellers in the 1960s, Llandovery has a lively theatre and several bookshops and provides a sensible base from which to explore the Tywi valley and the Dolaucothi gold mines.

Llandeilo, the next stop, has character, a magnificent setting and distinctive shops and services. It is also the departure point for Carreg Cennen and Dinefwr castles and the landscaped Dinefwr Park, managed by the National Trust.

So to Llandybie, which has an 18-hole golf course and the scenic Glynhir waterfall nearby.

The train now leaves the rural hinterland and

travels towards the old industrial centres of South Wales, Pontarddulais is attractively updated and spruce, and Llanelli, 15 minutes from Swansea, embraces a new leisure centre, a motor racing circuit and the Pembrey Country Park.

And so, almost four hours after leaving Shrewsbury, the journey along the scenic line Heart of Wales line terminates in the city of Swansea. The city is a place of paradox, the impersonal concrete of its post-war buildings offset by the warmth of its people, the ordered grid of its streets softened by the sweep of Swansea Bay. There is much to see and do here, and for the inquisitive visitor the journey's end is really the beginning..

THROUGH THE HEART OF WALES....... BY TRAIN

In any season
Climb aboard at
Shrewsbury town
Or Craven Arms, gateway
To the wilder country
Of Offa's Dyke

SHREWSBURY
CRAVEN ARMS
BUCKNELL
KNIGHTON
DOLAU
LLANDRINDOD WELLS
BUILTH ROAD

Over Teme and Wye
Past healing waters
Of Welsh spa wells

CILMERI
GARTH
LLANGAMMARCH WELLS

Through field and forest
Land of the Kite*

LLANWRTYD WELLS

And the blue, impassive
Hills of Wales

CYNGHORDY
LLANDOVERY

Through valley of Tywi

LLANDEILO

AMMANFORD
PANTYFFYNNON

And onward to the sea
At Swansea

LLANELLI

SWANSEA

TICKETS & TIMETABLES
Shrewsbury 01743 364041
Llandrindod Wells 01597 822053
Swansea 01792 467777
REGIONAL RAILWAYS

Milvus milvus: a predatory bird native to Mid-Wales

Focus on Wildlife

Radnorshire's Wild Places

Young Buzzard

If, like many visitors to Mid Wales, you have been attracted to the area by its natural beauty and landscapes, you may wish to take a closer look by visiting one of the Radnorshire Wildlife Trust's nature reserves.

The largest, and best known, reserve is Gilfach Farm, situated 3 miles north of Rhayader. The farm was occupied by a Radnorshire family until 1965. In 1988, the Trust bought the 383-acre reserve, including the Grade 2 listed traditional stone farmhouse, which had lain empty for 20 years. It was the first time in 200 years that the farm had come on to the market. The purchase of such a large and important area was a major success for a then recently formed Wildlife Trust, which was only a year old. The achievement was highlighted by a visit by His Royal Highness the Prince of Wales in 1989.

The real value of the reserve is the fact that it is a complete farm unit, extending from valley bottom to hill top, and containing river, meadow, pasture, woodland and sheep-walk. As well as creating an impressive landscape, this diversity of habitat allows the reserve to support a wide range of wildlife. The reserve is particularly rich in birdlife typical of the upland margins of Mid-Wales, such as the raven, red kite, buzzard, and wheatear. The woodlands contain wood warbler and redstart. The tumbling River Marteg is home to otter, dipper and salmon. Plants include the striking globeflower - a relative of the buttercup - and delicate mountain pansies can be seen in the pastures.

The Trust will open a visitor centre at Gilfach in 1995, whereupon a full range of facilities, including warden service, will be available. Details of opening times can be obtained from Tourist Information Centres or direct from the Wildlife Trust. There is already a nature trail in place and leaflets are available.

If you find yourself in the Painscastle area, there is an opportunity to visit the lake at Llanbwchllyn - the largest natural lake in Radnorshire. Lying in a shallow depression at the foot of a ridge of hills, this reserve is rich in aquatic plants and birds, such as the great crested grebe, reed warbler and pochard. Up until recently, the lake was used as a direct supply reservoir, but this is soon to be discontinued; a return to a more natural water regime is bound to benefit the wildlife of the lake.

The Trust also manage three woodlands in the county, all quite different from one another. Sidelands is a small ash wood near Penybont which was acquired by the Trust in 1982 as a gift from the owner. Here, it is possible to see the curious adder's-tongue fern and the common twayblade - a rare woodland orchid. It is also the home of woodland birds, such as the tawny owl. Bailey Einon, near Llandrindod Wells, is a charming woodland situated on the bank of the River Ithon. The reserve is rich in woodland flowers, such as early purple orchid, bluebells and yellow pimpernel. In spring, the wood is alive with bird-song, including that of the pied flycatcher, which raises its young here in the many nest-boxes the Trust has provided. These lovely birds, which belong to the same family as the more familiar robin, are common summer visitors to Wales. The male bird is an elegant black and white, the female a more subdued brown and white. Cefn Cennarth, near Pantydwr - the third of the Trust's woodland reserves - is an oak woodland, part of which is thought to have provided tan bark for the now defunct tanning industry in nearby Rhayader.

Presteigne is a charming town on the Radnorshire/Herefordshire border, and within walking distance of the town centre is the Withybeds reserve. Situated on the banks of the River Lugg, this small reserve has a circular walk with benches and a picnic area. The woodland is composed mainly of willow and alder trees, and flowers include marsh marigold and wood anemone. The river is home to otters, dippers and grey wagtail.

The rich wildlife of Radnorshire, and its beautiful and varied landscapes, are encapsulated in the Radnorshire Wildlife Trust's reserves, so please feel free to visit them.

If you'd like further information on locations and access; the Trust's address and telephone number is: Radnorshire Wildlife Trust, Warwick House, High Street, Llandrindod Wells, Powys. Tel: 01597 823298.

The Plight of the Red Kite

The red kite is a bird of the bare Welsh hills, a master of the air. It is one of Britain's rarest and most beautiful birds. Its plumage is an extraordinary palette of colours: russet-apple red, deep chestnut, bright lemon-yellow legs and a silvery white head. The kite's forked tail is a distinctive feature, as it soars and twists over its Mid Wales haunts - often referred to as Kite Country.

The kite feeds on small mammals, birds, carrion and earthworms. It sometimes covers more than 2,500 hectares in its search for food, effortlessly riding the thermals, taking the wind. The nest is built in the fork of an oak or sometimes a larch or a beech tree, where the hen bird will lay one to three eggs. A month later the eggs hatch and, for the next two months, the parent birds will work hard to feed the growing chicks. There is actually a shortage of food in some parts of Mid Wales, with the result that often only one young bird manages to leave the nest, and sometimes not even one, for nestling mortality is high.

The kite was formerly a numerous bird. In medieval times it was a common sight on the streets of London, and would sometime even feed from the hand. The 19th century saw the final demise of the kite with widespread persecution by landowners and gamekeepers. At the turn of the century only a handful of pairs clung to a precarious existence in the remote fastness of the hills of Mid Wales.

The population has slowly recovered since then, under determined protection measures. In 1991, a total of 77 pairs raised 63 young. But the attentions of egg collectors and, more importantly, the threat posed by poisoning of adults, have taken their toll. In 1989, at least 10 red kites were illegally poisoned. In 1990, more than eight nests were robbed with a further six nests robbed in 1991. Since before human memory, the landscapes of Mid Wales have been graced with the spectacular liquid flight of this graceful bird. Mid Wales is the last refuge for the Red kite and birdwatchers from all over Britain come to see this beautiful bird.

Red Kite

On 1 May 1994 the Kite Country project officer took up his new post based in the RSPB Wales office in Newtown. Tony Walker, formerly deputy director of the Campaign for the Protection of Rural Wales, was appointed project officer for the wide ranging partnership of local authorities, statutory bodies and RSPB which are involved in the Kite Country project.

It was the RSPB that originated the idea of a green tourism package for Mid Wales with the kite as its focus, and with the overriding aim of improving opportunities for visitors to gain a 'red kite experience', thereby reducing the risk of people disturbing nesting pairs by looking on their own initiative. When, in 1993, the red kite reached the target of 100 breeding pairs, it was decided, in conjunction with the Countryside Council for Wales, that the time had come when some of the veil of secrecy which had necessarily surrounded the species could be lifted and the opportunity created for people to be helped to see the bird more easily. The belief is that considerable education and conservation benefits could therefore come from this initiative. Given that the area in which the kite is

GWLAD Y BARCUD ~ KITE COUNTRY

Mid Wales is the last home of the native Red Kite population. The Kite Country project is setting up an environmentally friendly tourism package to allow the public to see the spectacular kite and other wildlife in Mid Wales.

At special feeding stations and through camera technology the public can see the kite without any risk of disturbance to it.

Kite Centres and exhibitions will be at Llanwrtyd Wells, Llandrindod Wells museum, the RSPB's Dinas reserve, Nant yr Arian forest centre near Aberystwyth, Llandovery and Gigrin Farm, Rhayader.

More information from: Kite Country, RSPB Office, The Bank, Newtown, Powys, SY16 2AB - 01686 624143

found has suffered serious economic decline in recent years, it was also felt by other partners, such as the local authorities and the Development Board for Rural Wales, that a more widely-based green tourism package, incorporating the red kite elements, will help provide a boost to the economy.

Now that the project has been launched and earlier ideas are metamorphosing into buildings, displays, brochures and so on, the effect of every proposal is being meticulously considered and monitored for any possible effects on the kites in particular but also on the environment in general. For example, a series of information centres around Mid Wales are being upgraded but the project is careful to reuse redundant buildings wherever possible. Work will be started shortly to renovate the cottage at Nant y Ffin on the RSPB Dinas reserve in the Tywi Valley and also to enhance the picnic area and provide better information about kites and other wildlife on site. At local authority centres in Llanwrtyd Wells and Llandovery, screens showing live and video pictures of local birds and wildlife will be installed and use will be made of up-to-the-minute video and computer technology to provide visitors with hitherto inaccessible glimpses into the secret life of some of our wild creatures.

The Kite Country project aims to promote the wildlife and environment of Mid Wales, and introduce visitors to the kite and its habitat. Visitor Centres at Llanwrtyd Wells, Llandovery, Llandrindod Wells and at the RSPB reserve near Rhandirmwyn offer a unique opportunity to observe the kite and other wildlife at close quarters. By employing two methods - through special technology and at feeding points - the project enables visitors to have a glimpse into the life of the kite without posing any threat of disturbance.

For further information write to:Kite Country, Bryn Aderyn, The Bank, Newtown, Powys SY16 2AB. Telephone: 01686 624 143.

Sports & Activities in the Heart of Wales

The unspoilt natural beauty of the Heart of Wales inspires many visitors to explore its great outdoors. There are activities to get the heart pounding - such as tough uphill trails for real mountain bike enthusiasts - and others to set the spirits soaring, including paragliding and abseiling. Walking, of course, is another great attraction, to be enjoyed at your own pace. And what better way to get the adrenalin flowing than taking up the challenge of canoeing in the very picturesque Wye Valley?

Here is a brief guide to just a few of the options open to those visitors looking for any kind of activity holiday or break in the Heart of Wales. For further details of the choices and facilities available, contact the appropriate Tourist Information Centres listed on page 143.

CLIMBING

MB Outdoor Pursuit Services

MB provide mountain-based activities for individuals, special needs groups, youth groups, independent and state schools and also various cadet forces. It is directed by Mark Brown who

has been involved in the outdoor pursuit industry since 1989. Courses are run for the beginner and the improver. The Introductory Course covers equipment, climbing and protection equipment, and basic techniques, all based on small climbs with lots of variations. The Improvers Course covers rope management, climbing techniques, emergency procedures, belay systems and leading.

The Introductory and Adventure courses. courses include abseiling. The Introduction course is suitable for the beginner or rock climbers wishing to familiarise themselves with the skill of descending fixed ropes. A Scrambling course is offered for those who are hillwalkers and wish to accomplish more adventurous routes or possibly a useful step

Rock Climbing

between hillwalking and rock climbing. The course includes route finding, group safety and effective belays through ropework. Other courses include a combination of basic mountain courses, abseiling, and river crossing. Team-building courses, mountain camping and kayaking trips are also part of the training offered. For further information telephone 01597 825671 or 0374 232380.

CANOEING

Wye Valley Canoe Centre

Established in 1968 and located at Glasbury in the beautiful Wye Valley, the Centre offers canoe hire and tuition to suit all grades and abilities. And you can take advantage of 100 miles of gently-flowing river. For more information ring 01497 847213

GOLF

Llandrindod Wells Golf Club

A superbly designed 18-hole course offering spectacular views, excellent hospitality and a variety of challenging holes - all at realistic prices. The clubhouse overlooks the lake, and facilities include bar, restaurant, changing rooms, showers and well-stocked gift shop. For more information ring 01597 823873.

Maesmawr Golf Club

Mid Wales Golf Centre, Caersws. For further information ring 01686 688303.

MOUNTAIN BIKING

Clive Powell Mountain Bikes

The unspoilt area around the Elan Valley, with its dramatic dams and miles of glorious open countryside, is the perfect retreat for mountain biking. Many of the byways and bridleways, once used for hauling peat and herding sheep and taking goods to market, now provide the challenge of lung-bursting climbs and exhilarating descents. Clive Powell Mountain Bikes offer a friendly service, with guides who will help you select routes to match your ability and experience. Advice and tuition are also available. For more information ring 01597 810585 or 811343.

PARAGLIDING

Paramania

The increasingly popular sport of paragliding originated ten years ago in the ski resorts of the Alps. With the development of

Paragliding

RADNORSHIRE
Leisure Services

Rhayader Leisure Centre

- 20m Swimming Pool & Spa Bath
- 2 Glass Backed Squash Courts
- Fitness Room
- 2 Sunbeds
- Snooker Room
- Lounge with Bar
- Cafeteria
- Main Hall

Excellent facilities for Parties, Weddings and Conferences etc

Rhayader Leisure Centre
Tel: (01597) 811013

Radnorshire Indoor Bowling Centre

Llandrindod Wells THE BEST BOWLS CENTRE IN WALES
COMPLEMENTING OUR INTERNATIONAL OUTDOOR RINKS

- 6 Superb Standard Rinks
- Excellent Bar & Catering Facilities
- Quality Changing and Toilets
- Fully Accessible to Disabled Players and Spectators
- Open All Year Round

Opening Times
1st Oct - 30th April - 10.00am -10.00pm
1st May - 30th Sept - 10.00am - 5.00pm
Coaching:- Courses for all standard of player can be arranged.

Radnorshire Indoor Bowling Centre (01597) 825014
or Radnorshire Leisure Services (01597) 823737

Wyeside Caravan and Camping Park ~ Rhayader

The site is situated alongside the River Wye in the small, attractive market town of Rhayader, where a new leisure centre has recently been opened. Within 100 yds of the site are the town's recreational facilities - including tennis courts, bowling green, children's play area, sports field and paddling pool. The site caters for 100 tents and 60 touring vans. A major improvement scheme has recently been carried out including a large new toilet/shower block. Warden's accommodation and extra hook-up points.

Bookings to the Warden Tel: (01597) 810183

modern materials and excellent training methods, it has rapidly evolved into an inexpensive, highly portable and relatively safe way to explore the air. Now you can experience the thrill of a bird's eye view of Mid Wales by visiting Paramania, who cater for everyone - from absolute beginners to experienced paragliders. For more information ring 01544 21375.

SPORTING BREAKS

Welsh Wayfaring Holidays
See Page 115
Mid Wales Leisure Breaks
This joint venture was formed recently by three established tourist attractions in the scenic Severn Valley. On offer are mini leisure breaks to suit all age groups, and the package includes two nights' accommodation and participation in three sports. If your accommodation is hotel-based, dinner is also included.

The sports comprise quad trekking (including instruction, safety briefing, helmets and waterproofs); golf (on a superb 9-hole course, with a practice range to try your skills beforehand); and clay pigeon shooting (where you will receive a brief introduction to the sport, personal instruction, and 50 clays and cartridges).

Each of the three attractions operating Mid Wales Leisure Breaks is a family-run business, and all visitors are guaranteed a warm and friendly welcome. For more information ring 01686 688303.

SWIMMING POOLS & SPORTS CENTRES

Canolfan Hamdden Bro Ddyfi
Machynlleth. Tel: 0654 703300
The Flash Centre
Salop Road, Welshpool. Tel: 0938 555952
Llanidloes & District Sports Centre
Llangurig Road, Llanidloes. Tel: 0686 412871
Llanfyllin & District Sports Centre
Llwyn Drive, Llanfyllin. Tel: 0691 648814

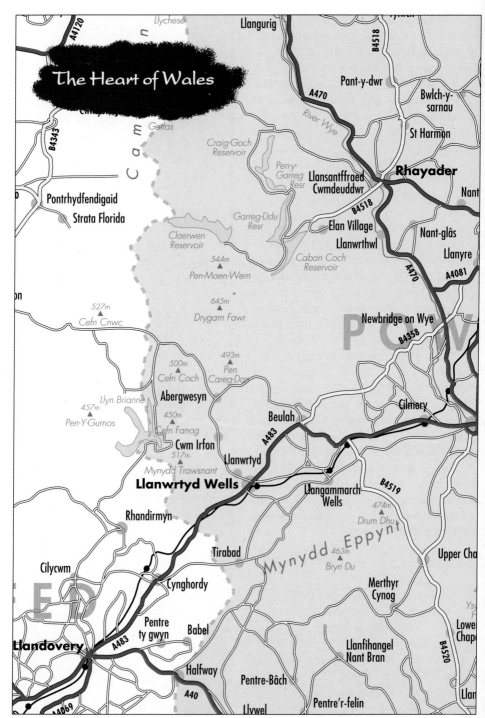

The Heart of Wales

Llychese

Llangurig

A4120

B4518

Pant-y-dwr

A470

Bwlch-y-sarnau

B4343

Cwm

Gettas

River Wye

St Harmon

Craig-Goch
Reservoir

Pen-y-
Garreg
Resr

Llansantffraed
Cwmdeuddwr

Rhayader

Pontrhydfendigaid

Strata Florida

Garreg-Ddu
Resr

B4518

Elan Village

Nant

Nant-glâs

Claerwen
Reservoir

Caban Coch
Reservoir

Llanwrthwl

Llanyre

A470

A4081

544m
Pen-Maen-Wern

527m
Cefn Cnwc

645m
Drygarn Fawr

Newbridge on Wye

POW

B4358

500m
Cefn Coch

493m
Pen
Careg-Dat

Llyn Brianne

457m
Pen-Y-Gurnos

Abergwesyn

450m
Cefn Fanog

Beulah

Cilmery

A483

Cwm Irfon

517m
Mynydd Trawsnant

Llanwrtyd

Llanwrtyd Wells

Llangammarch
Wells

B4519

Rhandirmyn

474m
Drum Dhu

Mynydd Eppynt

Tirabad

463m
Bryn Du

Upper Cha

Cilycwm

Cynghordy

Merthyr
Cynog

Ysv

Lowe
Chap

Pentre
ty gwyn

Babel

Llandovery

A483

Llanfihangel
Nant Bran

B4520

Halfway

A40

Pentre-Bâch

Pentre'r-felin

Llan

A4069

Llywel

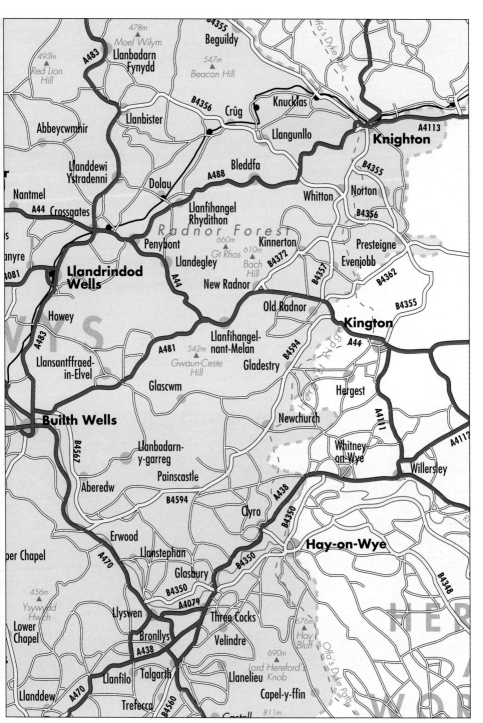

493m
Red Lion
Hill

478m
Moel Wilym

Llanbadarn
Fynydd

Beguildy

547m
Beacon Hill

A483

B4356

Crûg

Knucklas

Abbeycwmhir

Llanbister

Llangunllo

Knighton

A4113

Llanddewi
Ystradenni

Bleddfa

Dolau

A488

B4355

Whitton

Norton

B4356

Nantmel

A44 Crossgates

Llanfihangel
Rhydithon

Radnor Forest

Penybont

660m
Gt Rhos

Kinnerton

610m
Bach
Hill

B4372

Presteigne

Evenjobb

B4357

B4362

A4081

Llandrindod
Wells

Llandegley

New Radnor

A44

Old Radnor

B4355

Kington

Howey

A483

Llansantffraed-
in-Elvel

A481

542m
Gwaun-Ceste
Hill

Llanfihangel-
nant-Melan

Gladestry

B4594

A44

Glascwm

Hergest

Builth Wells

Newchurch

A4111

A4117

B4567

Llanbadarn-
y-garreg

Painscastle

Whitney-
on-Wye

Willersley

Aberedw

B4594

Clyro

A438

B4350

Hay-on-Wye

per Chapel

Erwood

Llanstephan

A470

B4350

B4348

Glasbury

456m
Ysywyyd
Hwch

B4350

A4079

Three Cocks

676m
Hay
Bluff

Lower
Chapel

Llyswen

Bronllys

Velindre

690m
lord Hereford's
Knob

Llanddew

A470

Llanfilo

Talgarth

A438

Llanelieu

Capel-y-ffin

Trefecca

B4560

811m

Abbey Cwm Hir

This remote village lies north-east of Rhayader and north-west of Llandrindod Wells, and is surrounded by woodland and hills. One of the first things you will notice upon entering the village is the interesting inn, named the Happy Union. The church opposite, built in 1836, has an interesting Light of the World window and the stone coffin lid of Abbot Mabli, who died in 1200.

The remains of the great abbey are the showpiece of this village. They lie among a scatter of elms and sycamores below the road in a river meadow. Only parts of the walls remain, with the bases of what must have been truly magnificent columns. It is said that the body of Llywelyn the last Prince was buried under the high altar. The abbey was founded in 1143 by Cadwallon ap Madog, a cousin of Rhys ap Gruffydd who was the founder of Whitland Abbey. The first monks were brought in from Whitland. Henry III plundered the abbey to avenge the misdirection of some of his soldiers by a friar, but it was the Welsh Owain Glyndwr who destroyed it, believing that the monks were spies for the English. At the Dissolution there were only three monks left there. The nave was the longest in Wales.

Aberedw

The village of Aberedw, which sits behind a massive, protective rock outcrop, is approached by twisting roads through the Wye Valley. Its square-towered church, St Cewydd, is tucked away from the road behind a row of cottages.

River Wye

Interesting features include an impressive porch and a 15th-century screen. A railway line, now closed, cuts through the remains of Llywelyn's Castle. Some of the stones of the castle were used as ballast when the line was built.

Builth Wells

This market town is set in a lush and beautiful section of the Wye Valley. It added Wells to its name after Lady Hester Stanhope, the niece of the younger Pitt, stayed nearby at the beginning of the 19th century. It was during the Victorian era that the town became a popular place to take the waters, first discovered during 1830. Today the waters are no longer consumed, but Builth has gained a new importance by becoming the permanent headquarters of the Royal Welsh Show. For one crowded week in summer every year it becomes the agricultural capital of Wales.

Livestock sales are also held regularly at the

Builth Wells

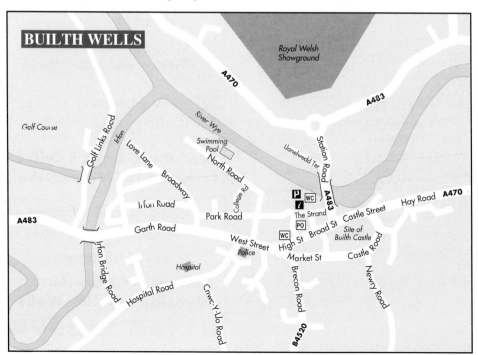

showground. The grounds lie across the river at Llanelwedd and are joined to the main town by a many-arched bridge. There is a pleasant tree-lined walk along the river bank. Overlooking the river on the south side is the flourishing Wyeside Arts Centre, which holds a regular programme of concerts, theatre, films and art exhibitions. The 14th-century church of St Mary's has been extensively rebuilt, and the remains of the once important castle are buried under grassy mounds behind the Lion Hotel.

Builth is a pony-trekking centre with hillsides above the Wye. To the south of Builth, the Wye runs through wooded hills which become dramatically rocky at Aberedw. It is popular with fishermen, and downstream it also attracts enthusiastic white-water canoeists. At Erwood, in a particularly fine section of the stream, a light bridge crosses the Wye. In the old days this was the place where the drovers urged their cattle through the shallows on their way to the markets of England. There are some beautiful walks on Mynydd Epynt, east of the B4519.

ATTRACTIONS & PLACES OF INTEREST

The Gallery

Well positioned opposite the Wyeside Art Centre, 'The Gallery' offers a good range of artists' materials and wonderful paintings to inspire even those with more modest talents. It is a treasure trove of old and new postcards, as well as gifts, quality greetings cards, toiletries and healthcrafts. There is also a fast, efficient photographic service for your holiday films. For further information telephone 01982 553518.

Wyeside Arts Centre

The Centre is housed in a fascinating Victorian Market Hall building on the famous Wye bridge in the centre of Builth Wells. Sympathetically converted to provide two

auditoria, a gallery, foyer and bars, Wyeside has a full year-round programme of arts & entertainment, films, exhibitions and workshops.

Wyeside's Live Show programme covers a wide variety of events, ranging from theatre, opera, and music from classical orchestras to comedy, ballet and modern dance and events for children. The emphasis is always on quality and value for money.

The gallery offers a wide range of exhibitions including, paintings, sculpture and photography, and the beautifully designed foyer craft cases feature a wide variety of craft-work, such as ceramics, wood, jewellery, glass, silk, leather, slate, and much more.

The cinema, recently expensively re-equipped to provide Dolby stereo sound and a bigger, brighter screen, offers the chance to see the best current releases as well as regular foreign/art house films.

Wyeside Arts Centre has recently been substantially remodelled with European funding, and its new foyer/coffee bar provides an attractive welcome to the Centre. The all-floor lift gives wheelchair access to the full range of the Centre's facilities, and infra-red sound enhancement systems are now installed in both cinema and live show auditoria. Hence Wyeside is well established as one of Wales' busiest and most exciting small arts centres.

The Royal Welsh Agricultural Society

When the Royal Welsh Agricultural Society put down its roots in Mid Wales in 1963, few could have foreseen the fantastic growth and development achieved by the Royal Welsh Show during the 32 years since.

The show had led a peripatetic existence for over half a century - the first was held in Aberystwyth in 1904 - alternating, with somewhat fluctuating fortunes, between North and South Wales. By 1963, however, the escalating costs of setting up in a different place year by year were almost too high to contain.

A - Z of the Heart of Wales

The site at Llanelwedd, Builth Wells, became available. Acquiring it was a wise and courageous decision by the leaders of the society. It was isolated in the middle of Wales but located in majestic countryside on the borders of Brecon and Radnor, two counties which welcomed the move wholeheartedly, giving it their unstinted support and setting out immediately to raise money to help finance improvements.

The society may not have realised it at the time, but this was the start of something big. Instead of the show going to the counties, the counties started going to the show to be featured in rotation, a development which quickly provided two key elements on which to build the future success of the TWAS - strong financial support from throughout Wales and an esprit de corps in the counties that bonds each of them firmly to Llanelwedd.

Over the years the counties have raised large sums of money and these have been utilised on buildings and infrastructure which have transformed the showground into one of the best in Europe - a continuing process involving an investment so far of over £5 million.

Llanelwedd has become the venue of the best-attended agricultural event in Britain. In 1963 there were 42,427 visitors. Last year, 229,711 people passed through the gates of the showground, now a mecca for farmers, livestock breeders, country-lovers and entertainment-seekers, mainly from Wales but also from the rest of the UK and other countries around the world.

Primarily a shop window for Welsh agriculture the show also fulfils an educational role and is a thriving centre for business as well. The main aim of the society, however, is to ensure that everyone going to the show, competitors and visitors - old and young alike - have a good time and enjoy themselves. It is this underlying theme of pleasure and enjoyment that has made the Royal Welsh such a popular attraction and the institution it has now become.

It costs more than £1 million to stage the

Royal Welsh Agricultural Show

event and when the 1995 show opens for four days on Monday, 24th July, visitors can expect to see some 6,000 animals, including the cream of Welsh livestock, and avenues packed with tradestands and shops. The show has special areas for forestry, the environment, outdoor pursuits, a huge flower and vegetable marquee, hundreds of stands for food, home-cooking, crafts, bee-keeping and poultry fanciers, to mention only a handful of the vast array of interests that in essence comprise many small shows within the principal event.

A brilliant programme of entertainment takes place in the main arena throughout the duration of the show - hours of interest and fun in a great holiday atmosphere.

All this activity has made the show a force in Welsh agricultural and rural business and its impact on the economy of Mid Wales is formidable. A recent study indicated that Llanelwedd, and the many activities now being

staged on the showground, generated an astonishing £24.1 million in the year to September 1993. Two-thirds of this figure - approximately £15.8 million - was motivated by the Royal Welsh Show itself and the local income generated by the showground was sufficient to support 147 direct and secondary jobs in Builth Wells and the surrounding area.

Visitors to Mid Wales should not miss the opportunity of coming to the Royal Welsh. which has special facilities at the International Pavilion for overseas guests.

Caersws

The main railway line to Shrewsbury and London from the Cambrian coast runs through this village, as does the main road from South to North Wales. Nearly 2,000 years ago the Romans had already recognised its strategic

position at the confluence of the Severn, Garno and Trannon rivers, and the outlines of the fort they built here can be traced near the railway station.

Caersws lies in the heart of typical Mid Wales country - rich meadows of the Severn backed by high hills not far from Newtown. The popular 19th century Welsh poet Ceiriog (John Hughes) was general manager of the little Van railway which ran from the main line at Caersws up to the rich Van lead mines.

At Caersws the railway leaves the Severn and follows the Carno valley westwards. Carno itself is a small village with three claims to fame. The first is in the inn with the extraordinary sign of the Aleppo Merchant. Some say it celebrates a local man who made a fortune out of Middle East trade. Others, less romantically, claim that the inn derived its name from the special pudding made here with liberal allowances of Middle East raisins. The second claim to fame is that Laura Ashley set up her first factory here in the village. And the third? You discover that just before you cross the bridge over the Severn and pass Maesmawr Hall - a fine example of oak-framed Jacobean black-and-white architecture. It is now a hotel. Many black-and-white timbered buildings, most of them farms, can be seen nearby in the upper Severn Valley.

Clyro

This peaceful village, situated off the A413, is just across the river from Hay-on-Wye. Some of the original 13th-century church survives, although it was rebuilt by J Nicholson in 1853. The Rev Francis Kilvert was curate here from 1865-1872, and his famous diary - selected and edited by William Plomer - opens with the last two of these years. The diary gives a charming picture of the Radnorshire people and countryside of Kilvert's day. A tablet to his memory can be found on Ashbrook House, where he lived.

A detour from the village takes you to Maesyronnel Chapel, which is set on a steep hillside, half a mile off the A438 near Glasbury (see Hay-on-Wye).

Elan Valley

See page 118

Erwood

Sited seven miles south of Builth Wells, on one of the most attractive stretches of the River Wye, this pretty little village was originally called Y Rhyd, meaning 'The Ford'. Erwood is associated with Llywelyn the Last, and the men of Edward I probably crossed the river here when they were hunting him. These days a bridge spans the river. It is believed that the concept of 'Punch' magazine was conceived here when Henry Mayhew stayed at the local

inn. Llangoed Castle lies two miles south-east and was rebuilt in 1911, though a south porch - dating from 1632 has been preserved.

ATTRACTIONS & PLACES OF INTEREST

Erwood Station Crafts Centre

This friendly and engaging centre displays the work of local craftspeople and artists, and it is housed in the former station of the Great Western Railway. Resident woodturner Alan Cunningham - a National Eisteddfod prize-winner - welcomes commissions from visitors, and also offers demonstrations and courses. The Centre is 6 miles south of Builth Wells, on the B4567, and is well signposted from the A470. For more information ring 01982 560674.

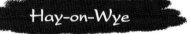

Hay-on-Wye

This charming market town, situated at the north-east corner of the Brecon Beacons National Park, is famous for its proliferation of second-hand bookshops. It is the gateway to the Welsh section of the Wye Valley, and is a typical border town. The Hay Bluff (2,219 ft) and Lord Hereford's Knob (2,263 ft) rise from the Black Mountains in the south.

At one time the town was a centre for the flannel industry, but it is now a local farming focus, where Clun and Kerry sheep are sold at the market. In the older part of the town the streets contain numerous little shops and are narrow and winding. The parish Church of St Mary dates largely from 1834, when it was rebuilt and enlarged. It still includes the early English southern entrance and 13th-century lower part of the square tower.

The first castle built here was a motte-and-bailey structure probably erected by a Norman knight called Revell in the 11th century. Traces of this can be found near the church, and the walk

Hay -on- Wye

Hay -on- Wye

HAY SWIMMING POOL

Hay Swimming Pool has been refurbished and is now a well equipped pool suitable for Beginners, Intermediate and most water sports and is available for all types of bookings. Public opening times are: Monday to Friday 6pm to 10pm ● Saturday 10am to 12.30pm and 2pm to 5pm. For more information please phone Hay Swimming Pool on **01497 820431.**

past here is known as Bailey Walk. A fine gateway, the keep, and parts of the walls are all that remain. Alongside this ruin is a privately-owned, early 17th-century Jacobean house which replaced the castle. The town itself has been described as a book-buyer's paradise. There are bookshops everywhere, hence it earned the reputation for itself as the second-hand book capital of the world. Other interesting shops, include those selling arts and crafts.

A spectacular mountain road south from Hay climbs to the 1,778 ft summit of the Gospel Pass in the Black Mountains before dropping down into the secluded Vale of Ewyas, Capel-y-ffin and Llanthony.

A few miles west of Hay, just off the A438, is Maesyronnen Chapel, which is believed to be the first in Wales. The stone long house, built in about 1696 and still filled with wooden furniture from the 18th and 19th centuries, was originally a secret meeting place of Nonconformist dissenters. The churchyard at nearby Llowes contains a fine Celtic cross.

Kerry

This quiet village situated on the edge of the Kerry Forest is about three miles east of Newtown. It has an ancient church with powerful Romanesque arcading. It is unique among the small churches of Wales for there is a complete description of its consecration in 1170. Kerry is one

of the few villages in Wales that has given its name to a breed of sheep. This large, sturdy, animal originated on the steep, close-cropped Kerry Hills to the south of the village. This is great grazing country, and great walking country as well. An ancient trackway runs the whole length of the hills, lifted high above the tumbled landscape, with fine views to the north.

Knighton

This little grey-stone town with a clock tower at its heart gives the impression that it is clinging desperately to the sides of the steep hill on which it has grown. The Saxons settled here first, then the Welsh arrived in 1052, to be quickly followed by the Normans soon after 1066. The Normans built the first castle - a timber structure on a mound situated behind the Smithfield and still called Bryn-y-Castell. The first stone castle was built on the other side of the town on the top of a hill in the 12th century, and the mound and remnants of a ditch are still visible.

Knighton's situation in the Teme Valley on the Welsh/English border, with the river's heavily wooded and mountainous left bank nearby, is delightful. The Welsh name for Knighton is 'Tref-y-Clawdd', meaning the Town on the Dyke, and Offa's Dyke runs all along the west side. This is a good starting point for walks along the 8th-century barrier put up by King Offa of Mercia as a dividing line between his kingdom and Welsh territory.

Offa's earthen wall and ditch ran for much of the length of Wales, from Chepstow to Prestatyn. As well as being a political barrier, the dyke served as a kind of customs point, controlling the movement of cattle and trade.

Remnants of this ancient earthwork can still be seen in many locations along the border. One of its best-preserved sections is at Llanfair Hill, about five miles north of Knighton, where the top

Knighton

of the bank to the bottom of the ditch measures 16 ft. The Offa's Dyke Heritage Centre, housed in an old primary school on West Street, gives information on short walks and has a small exhibition on the dyke's history. In the Riverside Park, behind the centre, a stone monument marks the opening of the one hundred and sixty-eight mile Offa's Dyke Long-Distance Path in 1971.

The Central Wales railway line runs through Knighton. The station is a little gem of Victorian-gothic railway architecture. This is because Sir Richard Green-Price, who released the land for the track, did so only on condition that he should personally approve the design of all stations, bridges, and other structures to be built in the area. The town contains a number of interesting old inns. The double-naved church, originally Norman, has been twice rebuilt. It is one of the few Welsh churches dedicated to an English saint, and the only one to St Edward.

The most picturesque street in Knighton is The Narrows, which runs uphill from the Clock

Tower. Right opposite the tower is the town's prettiest house - a narrow-fronted half-timbered building set back behind a delightfully paved courtyard. Every May the town holds a fair and an Agricultural Show and Carnival. Ruins of a Roman villa were discovered two miles outside the town in the hamlet of Stow during 1925.

Offa's Dyke Heritage Centre

Situated in West Street and open all year. For further information ring 01547 528192.

Offa's Dyke Antique Centre

Established in the border town of Knighton in 1987, the Centre supplies quality antiques and decorative items to the trade, interior designers, private collectors, holidaymakers - to anyone, in fact, who has an appreciation of old and beautiful things. Every effort is made to authenticate the genuine date of all pieces, and no new or reproduction item is ever knowingly offered for sale - a policy which has earned Offa's Dyke Antique Centre a national reputation and for several years has led to items being selected for Miller's Antiques and Collectibles Price Guide. However, this does not mean that everything here is expensive! On the contrary, items can cost as little as 50p, though of course a quality piece of furniture or antique could well run to several hundred pounds or more. There is also a great variety of things to see - from thimbles to teapots, drinking glasses to candlesticks, fine furniture to fine porcelain. Whatever your choice, a treasured item bought here will evoke fond memories of your visit to the beautiful Heart of Wales. For more information ring 01547 528635.

Llandinam

On more than one occasion, Llandinam has been awarded the title of 'Best Kept Village in Wales'. Colourful gardens line the A470 alongside the river Severn, and the black-and-white timbered houses of the village centre are set well back from the main road. The beautiful maintained little church overlooks the village, which is certainly worth a detour.

Llandrindod Wells

After the grey stone and slate so characteristic of Welsh towns and villages, Llandrindod Wells comes as a surprise with its towers, turrets, cupolas, balconies, oriels, colonnades, ornamental ironwork, loggias and balustrades. The town has magnificent gardens, parks, green banks and commons.

The town grew up around healing springs that rise here. Llandrindod emerged as a spa around 1670, but it did not reach its heyday until the second half of the 19th century. After a slow influx of visitors from the beginning of the century, William Grosvenor of Shrewsbury came to test the waters for himself. He was impressed and decided that the spa had a future, in which case hotel accommodation would become a necessity. He took a lease on the farm beside the little church up on the hill and converted it into the Grand Hotel.

After 1815 and the end of the Anglo-French wars, people began to visit Llandrindod in greater numbers, mostly staying at the Pump Room. The coming of the railway in 1866 took Llandrindod into its golden years. With the passing of a local enclosure act, building land became available, and the streets that now form the town centre were constructed. In 1871 a new church was built and at first called Christ Church, but later renamed Holy Trinity to avoid confusion with the Congregational Christ Church. In 1895 the old church up on the hill was restored and re-opened, and when the Church in Wales became disestablished from the Church of England it was here that the first Archbishop of Wales was elected.

Llandrindod Wells became the ecclesiastical capital of Wales, with the governing body of the Church in Wales holding its meetings here and other departments also finding the town a convenient half-way point between north and south for committee meetings. When

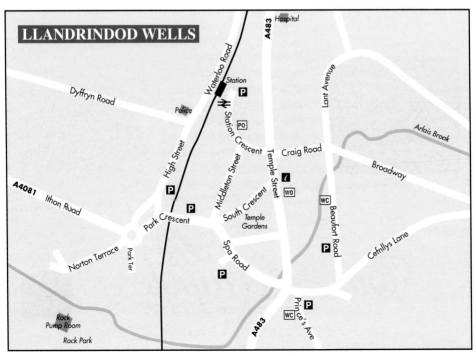

Victorian Festival - Llandrindod Wells

Llandrindod Wells was at the height of its popularity as a spa, 80,000 visitors would come to it in a season, with peers, judges, ambassadors, and other celebrities among them. Spa treatment went out of fashion, however, and Llandrindod declined. In the 1960s the Pump Room closed. The old Pump House has been refurbished, and you can still 'take the waters' here at Rock Park Gardens if you are brave enough. There is a local museum, a Welsh Crafts Centre and an interesting collection of bicycles in the Automobile Palace, in Temple Street.

A drama festival is held in the grandly named Albert Hall, at the beginning of May each year, and the atmosphere of yesteryear is re-created in the town every September for the week-long Victorian Festival, when everyone from the butcher to the baker dons the traditional costume of the period.

It is also a good touring centre for the attractive countryside around. The important Roman camp at Castell Collen, near Llanyre on the west bank of the Ithon, has been excavated and the lover of old and unusual churches will find some unexpected delights. For example, south of Llandrindod, the church at Disserth still retains its old box pews and on the road that leads north from Llandrindod to the Kerry Hills and Newtown, the church at Llanbister still has its 18th-century singing loft, where psalms were led by the village band. At the little church of Llananno, rebuilt in the 19th century, is a magnificent carved rood screen - a medieval masterpiece.

Little wonder that Llandrindod Wells is such a popular centre for holidaymakers wanting to discover the very heart of Wales.

ATTRACTIONS & PLACES OF INTEREST

Llandrindod Wells & Radnorshire Museum

Situated in the centre of Llandrindod Wells, the museum houses exhibits relating to the history of the old Mid Wales county of Radnorshire. Displays illustrate the largely rural

farming lifestyle of the area as well as the development of Llandrindod Wells as a country spa resort during the Victorian and Edwardian era. The museum also displays material relating to fine art, costume and the prehistoric, Roman and medieval history of the area, including the Roman fort of Castell Collen.

New for 1995 is the Red Kite Centre. Set on the museum's first floor, this exhibition highlights the lifestyle and successful fight back from the edge of extinction by Britain's most

Llandrindod Wells

beautiful bird of prey. The exhibition also includes a video and computer information station. For further information ring 01597 824513

Rock Park Spa
Tel: 01597 824729

Lear's Magic Lantern Theatre
Tel: 01597 824737

Llangammarch Wells

Situated at the confluence of the Cammarch and Irfon rivers, Llangammarch Wells is the smallest of the central Wales spa towns. It stands on the scenic Heart of Wales railway line, which links Swansea with Shrewsbury, and.its waters - once prescribed for certain heart conditions - were considered to be of the highest quality in Britain. The Pump Room still exists in the

grounds of the Lake Hotel.

Today's visitors come to the village for the fishing (the Irfon is a good trout river) and the tranquillity of the surroundings. Llangammarch stands at the northern end of Mynydd Epynt - a large, empty area of high moorland, where a road climbs up a steep-sided valley from the town. From the summit, there are glorious views northwards and eastwards across the mountains and borderlands of Mid Wales.

Llanwrtyd Wells

This little town dates from 1732, when Theophilus Evans - the grandfather of the historian Theophilus Jones - saw a frog disporting itself in the sulphurous waters. Since these waters apparently did not harm the frog, he thought that they might be worth trying as a cure for scurvy, from which he suffered. He began drinking them, found his condition improved,

Llanwrtyd Wells

Bog Snorkelling

and came to the conclusion that these were healing waters. So Llanwrtyd became a spa, and the wells at Dol-y-Coed still exist. Nowadays the little town is no longer visited by those in search of health, but by holidaymakers who come for the scenery and pony trekking - which is one of the specialities of the area.

Alongside the A483, on the outskirts of the town towards Builth Wells, is an old mill by a stream, which is now a shop selling Welsh tweed clothes and tapestries from the Cambrian

Woollen Mill next door. Free tours show how the wool is sorted, dyed, carded, spun and woven in the factory, which was originally founded to employ disabled ex-servicemen from the 1914-18 war. In 1927 the workshop was handed over to the British Legion. The Cambrian Woollen Mill is open to visitors every day except Christmas Day. For more information ring 015913 211.

ATTRACTIONS & PLACES
OF INTEREST

Welsh Wayfaring Holidays, Neuadd Arms Hotel

Situated in the picturesque spa town of Llanwrtyd Wells, this first-class hotel provides an ideal base for walking, pony trekking, horse riding, fishing, mountain biking, touring and a hundred and one other activities. This is also red kite country. For more details of the hotel's special package deals for holidays and breaks in this wonderful part of Mid Wales, ring 015913 236

New Radnor

New Radnor was founded by King Harold to replace Old Radnor as the administrative centre of the district. Walls and a castle protected it, and traces of the walls can be seen in a field at the end of a rough lane running off the Rhayader road on the left, just beyond the church. The castle stood behind the church, but nothing is left of it now except the mound. With the high summits of Radnor Forest behind and the Smatcher in front, both closing in on each other to the south-west, the town was only vulnerable from the east.

Water Street actually has a stream running down it, and small bridges to allow access to the houses. At its lower end is a monument somewhat resembling the Albert Memorial in London. This is a memorial to Sir George Cornwall Lewis, who died in 1863. He was a

baronet and MP for the borough from 1855 until his death, and it is thought that he might have become prime minister if he had not died when he did. The village is now bypassed by the A44, which makes it a very peaceful place.

Old Radnor

This village comprises a church, school, inn, a tiny group of council houses and a scatter of cottages. In pre-conquest times Old Radnor was a seat of local government and remained so until 1064. The church, which stands some 840 ft above sea level, has a battlemented tower and organ casing dating back to 1500, believed to be the oldest in Britain. The same is believed of the font, a massive circular block of stone with its top surface hollowed out to form a shallow bowl. The church also includes a wonderful medieval rood screen.

Painscastle

Painscastle is a compact village which took its name from Henry I's courtier, Pain Fitz John, who either built the castle or rebuilt in stone an earlier motte-and-bailey fortress.

Just one and a half miles west of Painscastle is the hamlet of Llanbedr, famous for its association with the Rev John Price, who was vicar here in Kilvert's time. Instead of living in his vicarage he preferred a shack of dry walling roofed with thin thatch!

Presteigne

This little town is situated on the west bank of the River Lugg. Presteigne is a border town, which takes its atmosphere and its architecture from the English county of Hereford and Worcester just across the river. Like so many of these small border towns, Presteigne grew up around a Norman castle. The castle has disappeared, but its site is now a public park known as The Warden. Broad Street has its Georgian houses, but the building which catches the eye is the half-timbered Radnorshire Arms

Hotel. It was built as a private house in 1606, became a coaching inn in 1792, and contains a priest's chamber, a Tudor doorway and secret passages. Presteigne was once the county town of Radnorshire until the reconstruction of the counties in 1972.

Radnor Forest

See page 119

Rhayader

Rhayader is a busy little crossroads town in the heart of the Welsh hills. The A470 north-south road meets the east-west A44 at Rhayader's neat little clock tower. The town is one of the leading livestock markets in Mid Wales. It has four main streets named after the chief points of the compass and still retains its

Elan Valley Reservoir - Dolymynach

LIVERPOOL HOUSE
Superb Accommodation

Bed, breakfast, optional evening meals. All rooms with TV, beverage facilities, hairdryer, clock/radio and most have en-suite. Private secure parking. Full fire certificate. WTB 3 Crowns.

East Street, Rhayader, Powys, LD6 5EA. Tel (01597) 810706

atmosphere of the 19th century. Its inns are even older, the oldest of them all being the Triangle, sited across the river in the district of Cwmdeuddwr, and is a partly weather-boarded building which dates from the 14th century. Nearly as old is the Cwmdeuddwr Arms on the Rhayader side of the bridge, which is of similar appearance.

Rhayader once had a castle. All that is left of it now is a large mound and a few stones in the angle between Church Street and West Street, high above the river. Upstream behind the castle is Waun Capel Park, from which a bridge leads over to a delightful sylvan riverside walk on the west bank. Extending from here to Llangurig is one of the prettiest reaches of the Wye, an eight-mile stretch of river with massive steep-sided mountains accompanying it on both banks. The scenery is really spectacular where the Marteg joins the Wye two and a half miles above Rhayader. The town was one of the centres of the Rebecca Riots last century, when men dressed as women and calling themselves Rebecca's Daughters smashed the turnpike gates as a protest against the heavy tolls. Today it is predominantly a tourist centre for the Elan Valley, which starts only three miles away. Rhayader is the first town of the Wye, so good fishing is guaranteed. The town has a small museum reflecting the bygone days of the region.

Cwmdeuddwr, although actually part of Rhayader, keeps its own identity and has its own church.

ATTRACTIONS & PLACES OF INTEREST

Elan Valley

This extensive series of man-made lakes in the heart of the moorlands west of Rhayader has become the major tourist attraction of Mid Wales. These reservoirs were built to supply Birmingham, 73 miles away, with water, but the city fathers were not afraid to spend extra money in making their dams, all of which are faced with fine stonework and are things of architectural beauty. The middle dam at Caban Coch is especially notable and is a magnificent sight when the waters overflow in winter. After the Second World War, the system was further extended by the construction of the vast Claerwen Dam, in a side valley of the Elan - a civil engineer's dream but a conservationist's nightmare. The history of the present dams is vividly re-told at the Visitor Centre which, located beneath the Caban Coch dam and close to the delightful 'model' village of Elan, was built in 1906-9 to house waterworks staff. The lakes form the basis of a 45,000-acre estate - an area renowned not only for the natural beauty of its open mountains, moors and oakwoods, but also for its prolific birdlife. The centre offers visitors a programme of guided walks and talks. Outside, overlooking the River Elan, is a statue of the poet Shelley (1792-1822), who lived with his first wife in a house now submerged beneath the waters of Caban Coch. When the reservoirs were constructed, eighteen farmhouses, a school and a church were destroyed.

The Elan Valley Visitor Centre is in Elan Village.For further information ring 01597 810880/810898.

Gigrin Farm Trail

For more information telephone 01597 810243

Marston Pottery

Lower Cefn Faes. Tel: 01597 810875

Rhayader Museum
Contact local TIC for further information.

Radnor Forest

Radnor Forest is not a true forest but an area of mountain split by numerous streams into a small, compact area of high, rounded hills. Although surrounded by hills of varying height, the Radnor Forest stands out as a distinct region on its own. A roughly triangular area about six miles in each direction, it is enclosed by main roads on all sides, giving the traveller fine views of almost every stream and hillside. Across its north side runs the main road from Knighton to Llandrindod Wells; to the south-west is the Kington to Rhayader A44 road; and to the south-east is part of the A44 to New Radnor.

Crags of Harley Dingle, views from Great Rhos or Black Mixen, Shepherd's Well, Rhiw Pool, and the spectacular Waterfall of 'Water-break-its-neck' are all of interest. The best natural waterfall in the region, 'Water-break-its-

Elan Valley Reservoir

neck' tumbles 70 ft into a dark wooded glen. It lies in the Warren Plantation on the west side of Ffron Hill, and can be easily reached by footpaths to the right of the A44 about one and a half miles west of New Radnor.

Welsh Royal Crystal

Welsh Royal Crystal is the Principality's own complete manufacturer of hand-crafted lead crystal products in tableware, stemware, presentation trophies and gift items. All production processes are undertaken on the one manufacturing site situated in Rhayader, in the heartlands of Wales.

Welsh Royal Crystal melts glass containing a lead content in excess of 30% (known as Full Lead Crystal) which is considered to be the best quality glass from which fine quality crystal glass products are made - weight and feel, definition of cutting and polishing brilliance are very much enhanced. Welsh Royal Crystal's range of products is traditional and the decoration combines classic florals (intaglio) with straight diamond cuts. A unique range of Celtic themes reflecting the design images of the Welsh Celtic heritage has been successfully introduced.

The design and supply of presentation trophies and gifts is an expanding area of the Company's business. Welsh Royal Crystal can number within its customer portfolio important corporate customers in Wales and is pleased to be associated with the Cardiff Singer of the World Competition sponsored by British Petroleum, the Young Welsh Singer Competition sponsored by the Midland Bank, the Welsh Woman of the Year sponsored by the Western Mail and HTV and "Achievement Wales Business Awards 1994" sponsored by the Daily Post and the Midland Bank. In addition to supplying our fine Welsh crystal to over 100 retail accounts in Wales, sales are increasing across the borders of the Principality into England, Scotland, Saudi Arabia, North America, Australia and Canada.

Welsh Crystal Workshops

Into South Montgomeryshire

Dylife

Dylife, high up on the eastern flank of the Plynlimon wilderness, is reached by the mountain road that winds up from Llanidloes, past Llyn Clywedog (a six-mile-long reservoir) and Staylittle. When you arrive here, you find no village - just an inn, some scattered houses and the remains of what was once one of the richest lead mines in Wales.

The Dylife stream drops into a spectacular gorge in one of the highest waterfalls in Wales - the Ffrwd Fawr. North of the mine area, a road leads off past the lonely lakes of Glaslyn and Bugeilyn into the heart of Plynlimon. On this road you will cross one of Wales' most memorable mountain roads, which climbs to a high point to offer a stunning panorama of mountain peaks. A short distance from the summit, in the direction of Machynlleth, look out for a viewpoint carved in dark slate. The late writer and broadcaster Wynford Vaughan-Thomas has been honoured by a memorial, unveiled in 1990, which must be the finest roadside viewpoint in Wales. At the road's high point, you can follow a rough track for a mile or so to the remote mountain lake of Glaslyn. There is a circular walk around the lake, which is part of the Glaslyn Nature Reserve.

Llanidloes

This attractive market town in Mid Wales is located at the junction of the Severn and Clywedog rivers, and in recent years has developed as a tourist centre. The town has a mixture of architectural styles, including Elizabethan, Georgian and Victorian. It owed its early prosperity to the lead mining in the

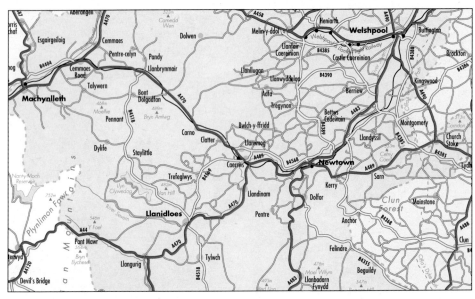

Dylife

surrounding hills and to the woollen trade. In the heart of the town stands the late 16th century timbered Market Hall. It has an open space beneath for the stalls, and a museum of local history is housed in the upper part. Such halls were common in the wool towns of Mid Wales, but this is the only surviving example. A tablet records the visit of John Wesley, who preached in the open air here at the hall. The 13th century church is impressive and the nave contains the graceful arches which were brought here from Abbeycwmhir, after the monastery there was dissolved in 1536.

The town boasts other half-timbered houses, and there are some interesting shop fronts. Royal Arms are displayed on the fascia of Hamer's butcher's shop in Long Bridge Street. The firm held the royal warrant for three successive reigns, and served eight royal families. A life-sized red lion lives above the door of an inn of that name, and outside Higgs' shop in Great Oak Street

Llanidloes

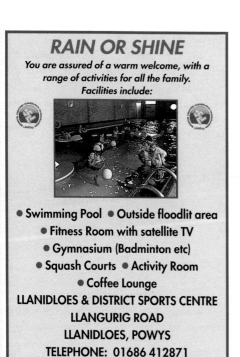
hangs a golden lamb to indicate the sale of woollen goods.

The Town Hall in Great Oak Street was a gift from the Davies family of Llandinam in 1908, while the Trewythen Hotel opposite has associations with the Chartist riots. Rioters took three policemen prisoner and held them captive there despite the efforts of fifty other constables to rescue them. They also took a former mayor prisoner and ransacked the hotel.

The town once had a castle, but only the site - where the Mount Inn now stands - remains. The wide main street leads down from the market hall to the bridge over the Severn. The left-handed road, immediately across the bridge, leads you into the hills to the north of the Clywedog. The Llyn Clywedog Scenic Trail is two and a half miles long and starts above the car park on the Staylittle road. It is possible to make a circuit of the lake. The route takes you through the vast Hafren Forest, which spreads over from the Clywedog valley into that of the infant Severn.

The forest stretches far up the eastern slopes of Plynlimon, and the Forestry Commission has designated some attractive trails, including the Source of the Severn Walk, the Cascades Forest Trail and the Blaenhafren Falls Walk. The circuit of the lake eventually brings the motorist back into the Clywedog valley and to the area around the dam itself. Good fishing, enjoyed by a former US President during his holiday in the region, is available in the lake, under the auspices of the local angling club.

The small Bryn Tail Lead Mine site near the dam has been cleared for a well-signed industrial archaeology trail. To the east of Bryn Tail are the remains of the Van Lead Mine - once the most profitable in the region. Glyndwr's Way, part of a 121-mile walk across Powys from Knighton to Machynlleth, also crosses here.

ATTRACTIONS & PLACES
OF INTEREST

Llanidloes Museum

Situated on the ground floor of the Town Hall, Great Oak Street, the museum houses exhibits relating to the long history of this ancient market town, with its timber-framed black and white Old Market Hall. Artefacts of particular interest relate to the history of mining in the area and to the Chartist revolt of 1839. For further information contact the local Tourist Information Centre (01686 412605).

Into South Montgomeryshire

The Nature Gallery

This gallery, situated in Llanidloes, is a fascinating shop filled with gifts and prints and original paintings, which all share nature as a common theme, and a different local artist is exhibited each month. The shop is run by Sue Whitehead, herself an artist, who also runs the Mid Wales Bird Hospital with her husband. The Hospital, which is funded only by the shop and donations from supporters, cares for and rehabilitates those wild birds injured on the roads and elsewhere. A visit to the shop is therefore not just a pleasure in itself, but anything purchased helps maintain a worthwhile cause.

The Mid Wales area is a bird-watching paradise, containing as it does the rare red kite and most other birds of prey, including visiting ospreys. Having a varied habitat it is also attractive to many species of waders, ducks and other small native species. For further information telephone 01686 413117.

Montgomery

Montgomery is situated within a mile of the Shropshire border. It has a small square with an 18th-century town hall, Georgian houses of red brick, old inns, and half-timbered Elizabethan and Jacobean houses.

Behind the square rises the castle hill, on which Roger de Montgomery built his first stronghold in the 13th century, and from which he launched his attack on the lands of the Welsh to the west. The position of Montgomery, on a high ridge ending with a crag to the north, made it a key point in the politics of the border.

Montgomery Church is mainly 15th century, with a splendid rood screen and richly carved tombs of the Herbert family. In the graveyard is the Robber's Grave - John Davies was convicted of murder in 1821 and was buried in this corner. He swore that he was innocent, and declared that, in proof of it, nothing would grow on his grave

for over a hundred years.

Beyond the church there are traces of the old walls, with a view out towards England and the east. Offa's Dyke ran close to the town, and its course can be traced from Montgomery to the Long Mountain behind Welshpool. Remains of the Dyke are preserved in Lymore Park, east of the town.

ATTRACTIONS & PLACES OF INTEREST

Montgomery Castle

For more details contact the local Tourist Information Centre.

Old Bell Museum

For more details contact the local Tourist Information Centre.

Machynlleth

One of the most agreeable of all Welsh towns, particularly for its enchanting position in the Dovey Valley, which is a beautiful natural feature of Mid Wales. It has been an inhabited site since the early Iron Age. Owain Glyndwr made it the capital of Wales, and he was proclaimed king here at a parliament in 1404; the present Institute is traditionally his Parliament House. Because of Machynlleth's position at the junction of several old coach roads, and as a great sheep-trading centre, the town had twenty-four inns in the 19th century. Four inns, the haunt of anglers fishing the Dovey, still cluster round the clock tower which marks the centre of the town. There are 17th, 18th and 19th-century houses in the street called Maen Gwyn, and near the clock tower is Royal House, where the future Henry VII is said to have stopped in 1485.

ATTRACTIONS & PLACES OF INTEREST

Dyfi Centre

Part of the Tourist Information Centre. Tel: 01654 702401.

Newtown

Machynlleth

Newtown, in the centre of the Upper Severn Valley in Mid Wales, is the market town for a broad and fertile area. The wide central street leads down to the river and pleasant riverside promenade.

The old church stands near the bridge. The fine tower remains, but a new church was built in 1847 on the main road. The original church, however, has in its graveyard the tomb of Newtown's most famous son, Robert Owen. He was born here in 1771, and was a pioneer of enlightened capitalism in his New Lanark mills in Scotland, but gained his greatest fame as one of the fathers of the cooperative movement in Britain. He was also the founder of nursery schools. There is a Robert Owen Museum in Broad Street, and a small textile museum in one of the old hand-weaving factories in Commercial Street.

In the centre of the town several interesting architectural styles crowd the main shopping streets, including the ornate Barclays clock tower and a brick-and-timber W H Smith, restored to its early 20th century elegance and housing a small exhibition about the famous firm on its upper floor. Older buildings can be seen in the side streets and squares leading towards the river.

Newtown has benefited by the establishment of new industries, including a Laura Ashley factory. It still, however, still retains an air of a busy market town. Next to the station is the large Royal Welsh Warehouse where, in 1859, Pryse Jones started the world's first mail-order scheme, selling Welsh flannel products. The beautiful 32-acre Dolerw Park lies over the river from the town, and is reached by a new footbridge across the Severn. Newtown also has its own little theatre which offers a varied programme of opera, drama and dance.

Behind the town, on the road to Llanfair Caereinion, is the church of Bettws Cedewain, with its 14th-century roof. From Bettws you can traverse the complicated and narrow roads to Gregynog Hall, four miles north of Newtown. It was the home of the Davies sisters, who made it a

Into South Montgomeryshire

centre of the arts and music in the years after the First World War. Here they established the Gregynog Press, producing editions much sought after by lovers of fine printing, and accumulated the remarkable collection of works by French impressionists which is in the National Museum at Cardiff. The Gregynog Press has been reinstated with assistance from the Welsh Arts Council.

About three miles north-east of Newtown, along twisting, narrow lanes off the A483 near Abermule, are the remains of Dolforwyn Castle, a Welsh fortress built by Llywelyn ap Gruffudd in 1273.

ATTRACTIONS & PLACES OF INTEREST

Davies Memorial Gallery
Tel: 01686 625041
Newtown Textile Museum
For further details contact the local

Tourist Information Centre.
Robert Owen Memorial Museum
For further details contact the local Tourist Information Centre.

W.H. Smith Museum
High Street. Tel: 01686 626280

Dolforwyn Castle
For further information contact the local TIC

Theatr Hafren
Llanidoes Rd. Tel: 01686 625007

Welshpool

A bustling market town with well-ordered streets which looks and feels more English than it does Welsh. There are half-timbered Tudor buildings and Georgian architecture to be

Newtown

Welshpool

found in this borderland town. It stands on the Montgomery Canal and visitors can enjoy trips along part of the canal's restored section.

Welshpool has two noteworthy churches. St Mary's stands on high ground overlooking the town, and dates back to the 13th century. The other church is located to the west of the town centre and commands views over the Severn Valley. The Powysland Museum has many interesting relics of the region, the most notable of which is an Iron Age shield.

.Welshpool's crowning glory is Powis Castle, about 1 mile south-west of the town..

ATTRACTIONS & PLACES OF INTEREST

Powis Castle & Gardens
For opening hours telephone 01938 554336

Powysland Museum & Montgomery Canal Centre
Tel: 01938 554656

Welshpool & Llanfair Light Railway
Tel: 01938 810441

See the other Lily Publications'
Premier Guides in this series:

Pembrokeshire

Cardiganshire

Swansea Bay & The Gower

Cardiff

Isle of Man

Tour 1

Brecon-Builth Wells-Llangammarch Wells-Llanwrtyd Wells-Llandovery-Brecon

64 miles

From Brecon take the A438, signposted Hereford, and within a quarter of a mile you will reach the Bulls Head Hotel. Turn left then on to the B4520 Upper Chapel road. After a short distance you will pass the cathedral. Continue through pleasant hill scenery, following the road into the **Honddu Valley** and on to Lower Chapel. After Upper Chapel, on the southern edge of the **Mynydd Eppynt** hills, remain on the Builth Wells road. Turn right after Upper Chapel onto the B4520. At the summit (1,370 ft) there are outstanding views over the hills before the long descent into **Builth Wells**. Turn left, joining the A483 Llandovery road, and cross the **River Irfon**. Continue along the valley until you reach the village of **Garth**. From Garth turn left on to the unclassified **Llangammarch Wells** road. Just outside Llangammarch Wells turn right for **Llanwrtyd Wells**, crossing the Afon Cammarch. After about a mile turn left, following the railway into **Llanwrtyd Wells**, then turn left on to the A483 Llandovery road.

There is a gradual climb up to the edge of **Crychan Forest** and to the 950 ft road summit of the **Sugar Loaf** (1,000 ft), which stands at the head of the **Bran Valley**. The conical shape of the hill is revealed on your descent to

Abergwesyn Pass

Llandovery. In the town there is an unclassified road on your right, signposted Rhandirmwyn. This road leads for 12 miles along the very pleasant **Tywi Valley**. There is spectacular hill scenery along the road as you near the end of the valley and approach the **Llyn Brianne Reservoir and Dam**. From the viewing point a narrow road leads high above the shores for seven miles into the **Tywi Forest**. Situated between the rivers Tywi and Bran, is the pleasant market town of Llandovery, with its ruined Norman castle. From the town take the A40 towards Brecon, which takes you through the deep, wooded valley of the **Afon Gwydderig**.

Beyond Trecastle you will follow the River Usk for the short distance to **Sennybridge**. After the village turn right onto the A4057, and at Defynnog bear left onto the A4215 Merthyr road. Continue along the **Senni Valley**, which will give you fine views ahead of **Fan Frynych** (2,047 ft) and other Fforest Fawr hills. After 2¾ miles turn left at the signpost for the Mountain Centre on to a narrow road crossing the **Mynydd Illtyd** (1,100 ft). To the right there are sweeping views of the Brecon Beacons, with the main summits of **Pen-y-Fan** (2,906 ft) and **Corn Du** (2,863 ft) clearly visible. The **Mountain Centre** is a Beacon Beacons National Park information centre, with a viewing gallery and picnic area. From the centre the road gradually descends, offering fine views of the **Black Mountains**, and on reaching the A40 turn right for Brecon.

Tour 2

Brecon-Merthyr Tydfil-Talybont-Crickhowell-Brecon
63 miles

Leave Brecon on the Llandovery road (A40) and cross the **River Usk**. After about 1 mile cross the **River Tarell** and at the roundabout take the second exit. Take the next turning left, signposted Mountain Centre. The road then gradually climbs up to a moorland region which reveals excellent views (to the left) of the Brecon Beacons, with the summits of **Pen-y-Fan** (2,906 ft) and Corn Du (2,863 ft) clearly visible.

The route continues on past the entrance to the Mountain Centre on the left, which contains models and information on the Brecon Beacons National Park. There is also a picnic site here. After a mile you will come to a crossroads; turn left onto the A4215, with **Fan Frynych** (2,047 ft) rising straight ahead. After 3 miles the road descends into the **Tarell Valley**; turn right on to the A470, signposted Merthyr. The road then is an easy ascent leading to a summit of 1,440 ft, with **Fan Fawr** (2,409 ft) ahead. On the left after ½ mile is the starting point of footpaths to the main peaks. From here, the road then begins the descent along the wooded **Taff Valley**, passing three reservoirs before reaching the edge of Merthyr. Continue to **Cefn-coed-y-cymmer** on the outskirts of **Merthyr Tydfil** and then turn left on to the Pontsticill and Talybont road. The road passes the gorge of the **Taf Fechan**, which is on the right, and a mile and a quarter later, after passing under a railway bridge turn left. A short detour can be taken from here to the ruins of 13th-century **Morlais Castle** by turning right after passing under the railway bridge.

The main tour then continues through **Pontsticill**, and at the end of the village keep left to follow the shores of the **Taf Fechan Reservoir**. Ahead there are distant views of the lower Brecon Beacon summits. After 2¾ miles the route turns right, but for the **Neuadd Reservoirs** below the Beacons go straight on. The main route crosses the river before passing a picnic area. On the ascent to a 1,400 ft summit, the site of the former **Torpantau Station** - 1,350 ft above sea level - is passed on the left. At the top there are views to the left of **Craig y Fan-ddu** (2,224 ft) and **Craig y Fan** (2,502 ft) before a long steep descent through woodland to the **Talybont Valley**. With 2,000 ft hills on the left and the prominent 1,806 ft - peak of **Tor-y-Foel**

Mynydd Illtyd

ahead, the drive follows the two - miles - long Talybont Reservoir. About 1¼ mile beyond the reservoir, turn right - no signpost - into **Talybont** village.

The road then crosses the restored **Brecon and Abergavenny Canal**, which is open for pleasure craft from Brecon to Newport. Turn right on to the B4558 - no signpost - and beyond the village follow the signposts for Llangynidr and Crickhowell. The road continues along the lovely wooded **Usk Valley**, with views of the canal on the right. Beyond the canal bridge at the edge of **Llangynidr**, turn right on to the B4560 Beaufort road. Climb through sharp bends to an altitude of 1,460 ft from where the views across the Usk Valley to the Black Mountain are magnificent. The major hills to be seen from here include **Mynydd Llangorse** (1,700 ft), **Pen Cerrig-Calch** (2,302 ft), **Pen Allt-Mawr** (2,360 ft), **Crug Mawr** (1,805 ft) and the famous **Sugar Loaf** (1,955 ft) above Abergavenny. Continue past a quarry and then turn left on to an unclassified road signposted Crickhowell. For a detour to view from 1,694 ft, continue the ascent on the B4560 for ½ mile. The main drive continues by descending gradually before recrossing the canal at **Llangattock**. Keep straight ahead for the end of the village and turn left on to the A4077; then turn right to cross the Usk by an attractive bridge into **Crickhowell**.

At Crickhowell there are several Georgian houses and a restored 14th-century church with a shingled spire. After visiting the town leave on the A40 Brecon road and continue through attractive valley scenery. After 2¾ miles the road passes a right turn which leads to the hamlet of **Tretower**, with its picturesque manor house and ruined castle. After 2½ miles the drive climbs to **Bwlch**, where there are good views of the **Usk Valley**. Beyond the village, at the war memorial, turn right on to the B4560 Talgarth road and continue along high ground below **Mynydd Llangorse** (1,700 ft). To the left is **Llangorse Lake**, which is the second largest natural lake in

Wales. At the end of Llangorse village turn left on to the little country road (which takes you towards Brecon), shortly after passing a road to the lakeside. After 1½ miles turn left across a bridge and pass through **Llanfihangel Tal-y-Llyn**. After 2½ miles, turn left. After ½ mile turn right on to the A40 to return to Brecon alongside the Brecon and Abergavenny Canal.

Tour 3

Rhayader-Elan Valley-Devil's Bridge-Llangurig-Rhayader
60 miles

Rhayader, in the upper Wye Valley, is a popular touring and pony trekking centre and an ideal starting point for a pleasant day's ride. Within easy reach are woodlands, reservoirs, river valleys with waterfalls, and mountain views.

Leave Rhayader on the B4518 for the highly attractive **Elan Valley** reservoirs. These were built from 1892 onwards for Birmingham Corporation. At the edge of **Elan** village, continue straight on and climb to the **Caban Coch Dam and Reservoir**. Follow the road round to the **Garreg-Ddu** viaduct; then turn left to cross it on the road to the **Claerwen Reservoir**, which was opened in 1952. Continue through pleasant woodland, with the remains of the **Dol-y-Mynach Dam** on the left, and drive along the attractive **Claerwen Valley**. Turn right to reach the **Claerwen Dam**. Return along the same road to the Garreg-Ddu viaduct and turn left, following the wooded shores of **Garreg-Ddu Reservoir**. At the end is a short, winding climb which leads to the **Penygarreg Dam** and Reservoir. Beyond is the dam of **Craig Goch Reservoir**. The water stretches out beside the road as the drive passes through pleasant moorland before climbing to turn left on to the Aberystwyth road .

Continue along the valley beside the River

Elan to reach the 1,320 - ft summit, then make the long descent into the deep and wild **Ystwyth** Valley. After 3¾ miles, the road passes the extensive remains of former lead and silver mines. After **Cwmystwyth** the road then climbs again to join the B4574 Devil's Bridge road. Following a small climb, the road then gives views of the **Rheidol Valley** ahead and the deep **Mynach Valley** on the right. The descent continues to **Devil's Bridge**, where there are three bridges spanning the deep **Mynach** gorge and spectacular waterfalls cascading through the rocky chasm. Turn sharp right on to the A4120 Ponterwyd road, crossing Devil's Bridge and keeping high above the Rheidol Valley. After 2¾ miles turn right on to the B4343 Dyffryn Castell road, which climbs to 1,000 ft high above the main A44 road. Later take the A44 towards Llangurig to make the long, gradual climb out of the **Castell Valley**. **Eisteddfa Gurig**, at the 1,400 ft summit, is the starting point of several beautiful walks and pony trails to the 2,470 ft summit of **Plynlimon**. This famous mountain is the source of the River Wye; and the River Severn rises three miles farther north. On the long descent the road follows the **River Tarenig** before the River Wye joins it from the left. There are good views of the river as the drive approaches **Llangurig**, a pretty village attractively situated at over 900 ft. Bear right, with Rhayader signposted on to the A470. This very pleasant road follows down the Wye Valley back to Rhayader.

Tour 4

Llandrindod Wells-Newton-Rhayader-Llandrindod Wells

65 miles

The beautiful Victorian spa town of Llandrindod Wells is a convenient starting point for this drive which takes you through wooded river valleys overlooked by mountains.

Leave Llandrindod Wells on the A483 Newtown road and cross the **Ithon** before the Cross Gates roundabout. At the roundabout keep straight on (signposted Newtown). The road then follows along the river on the approach to the village of **Llanddewi**, and then runs through the pleasant winding valley past the edge of the villages of **Llanbister** and **Llanbadarn Fynydd**. After passing the New Inn, turn right on to the road signposted Dolfor, which gradually climbs to 1,500 ft of moorland with good all-round views. Then follow the B4355 Newtown road. The higher ground to the right is the source of the **River Teme**, while the River Ithon rises on the left. The road then descends downhill and offers some fine views. At Dolfor, turn right on to the A483, then right again on to the road which goes past the church. Continuing straight on, the road now climbs to 1,200 ft and offers magnificent views over Newtown, the Severn Valley from Caersws to Welshpool, and the surrounding hills. To the east are the **Long Mountain and Breidden Hills**, and in the far distance **Cader Idris** and the **Aran** and **Berwyn** mountains - all over 2,700 ft high.

After a long descent, turn left at the crossroads on to the A489 to **Newtown**. This is an important market town, once famous for the manufacture of woollens, and is worthy of a stop. At the junction with the A483, turn left for Llandrindod Wells. After leaving the town, the drive takes a long, winding ascent past **Dolfor** to a 1,150 ft summit. Proceed straight on for 2½ miles, following the signs for Bwlch-y-Sarnau. The road crosses the River Ithon, and follows its tributaries upstream through pleasant country to a 1,500 ft level. There are fine views before the road bears right to reach the hamlet of **Bwlch-y-Sarnau**. Continue, and after a short distance descend along a narrow road to the **Clywedog Brook** in its pleasant valley. Continue through wooded hills - part of the **Sarnau Forest** - and at the T-junction turn right towards Rhayader. The road again climbs through woodland, this time to

1,370 ft. Further outstanding views are offered west towards Rhayader and the hills surrounding the Elan Valley reservoirs. Then descend to a T-junction and turn left. After about 1 mile, turn right and continue to Rhayader. Follow the A470 into the town centre and turn left on to the Builth Wells road. Follow the attractive, partly-wooded valley of the River Wye. At **Newbridge-on-Wye**, which is a good fishing centre near the confluence of the Wye and Ithon, turn left on to the B4358 Llandrindod road. After about 2 miles go straight on to the A4081, and shortly beyond the village of **Llanyre** bear right to return to Llandrindod Wells.

Tour 5

Builth Wells-Hay-on-Wye-Kington-Builth Wells

64 miles

Leave the pleasant market town of Builth Wells on the A470 Abergavenny road, following the tree-lined River Wye. At **Erwood**, there are good views ahead of the **Gwent Black Mountains** and **Waun Fach** (2,660 ft), the highest point, on the approach to **Llyswen**. Drive for about ½ mile beyond the village and turn right to ascend before entering the **Llynfi Valley**, with the distinctive mountain shape of the **Mynwydd Troed** (1,997 ft) ahead. At the T-junction turn right on to the A438, and on entering **Bronllys** turn left on to the A470 towards Talgarth. Within ½ a mile **Bronllys Castle**, dating from c1200, can be seen on the left. Continue into **Talgarth** and turn left on to the A4078 (Three Cocks and Glasbury road). After 2 miles turn right on to the A438 Hereford road and drive through **Three Cocks** (or Aberllynfi), to the edge of Glasbury. Then follow the B4350 Hay road, following the Wye Valley to Hay-on-Wye. Turn right on to the B4348 Bredwardine road, which takes you into the county of Herefordshire at **Cusop**. After 2¾ miles turn right (signposted Peterchurch) and

continue along an undulating road with views to the left before passing **Merbach Hill** (1,045 ft). Ahead is the **Golden Valley**. At the edge of Dorstone bear left, and after a short distance you will pass a church which has a 13th century tower arch. Carry on for ¼ a mile to **Bredwardine**, and climb the steep **Dorstone Hill** (824 ft). Fine views to the west from the steep descent encompass Hereford and Worcester and also the Wye Valley. A road on the left, signposted Arthur's Stone, climbs to over 900 ft. About ¾ of a mile further on to the B4352 Hay road, and after a short distance enter Bredwardine.

Turn right at the Red Lion Hotel on to the Staunton road. Cross the River Wye by an old bridge, then turn left and follow the wooded banks of the river. After 1½ miles, turn left again on to the A438 Brecon road into the village of Letton. After 1½ miles, carry straight on along the A4111, signposted Rhayader. The picturesque village of **Eardisley** has many black-and-white-houses and a Norman church with a finely-carved font. From here there is a long, gradual climb before the descent to **Kington**, on the **River Arrow**. Turn left into the town on the A44 and continue to the far side. Pass an old church which contains a good 13th-century chancel. Follow the **Cynon Brook** between **Hergest Ridge** (1,394 ft) and the conical **Hanter Hill** (1,361 ft) on the left and **Bradnor Hill** (1,284 ft) on the right. After about 2 miles you will reach the Welsh border and cross into the county of Powys. The picturesque **Stanner Rocks** stand out on the right. Beyond Walton, on the approach to New Radnor, there are views of the **Radnor Forest** area. Enter the village and then turn left below the earthworks of a former castle. After about ½ mile, turn right, and follow a deep valley by the name of **Harley Dingle**, which cuts through the Radnor Forest. On the left is **Fron Hill** (1,916 ft) with the 2,166 ft summit of **Great Rhos** behind it, and on the right are **Great Creigiau** (2,100 ft) and **Whimble** (1,965 ft). About 1 mile farther on, below the **Mynd** (1,530 ft),. a footpath on the

Dylife - Wynford Vaughan Thomas Memorial

right leads to woodland surrounding the 70 ft high **Water Break-Its-Neck waterfall**. After 2 miles, at the Forest Inn, turn left on to the A481 Builth road, which passes **Llynheilyn** on the left. Continue through pleasant hill country region, crossing the **River Edw** at **Hundred House**. After 4 miles rejoin the Wye Valley, which then leads back to Builth Wells.

Tour 6

Llanidloes-Machynlleth-Llanidloes

56 miles

Leave Llanidloes on the B4518 Llyn Clywedog road and cross the River Severn, turning left to follow the **Clywedog Valley**. After about 2 miles, with views of the 1,580 ft **Fan Hill** on the right, turn left. Cross the valley before making the ascent past the **Clywedog Dam**.

There is a viewing area on the right, and the 237 ft dam opened in 1968, is the highest in Britain. There are further views of the reservoir before the drive enters the extensive **Hafren Forest**. At the T-junction turn right on to the Llanbrynmair road. After 2¾ miles you will reach the edge of Staylittle and then turn left on to the B4518. In ¾ of a mile turn left on to the unclassified Machynlleth road. Take care as the road is unprotected and after a short distance passes high above the deep, V-shaped gorge of the **River Twymyn** on the right. Continue to the former mine workings at the remote hamlet of **Dylife**. A long climb to 1,700 ft high moorland gives wide, distant mountain views.

On the descent the views are even more impressive. Beyond a range of 2,000 ft hills above the **Dovey Valley** are the distant summits of **Cader Idris** (2,927 ft), 14 miles away, and **Aran Fawddwy** (2,970 ft), 16 miles away and the higher of the two Aran mountains. This is the highest Welsh summit outside the Snowdon Mountain range. After a long, easy descent, keep straight on at all road junctions before dropping more steeply into the wooded **Dulas Valley**. Follow this through to the pleasant market town of **Machynlleth**, which lies in the **Dovey Valley** and is dominated by its massive clock tower. Leave the town on the A489 Newtown road and pass through **Penegoes** before re-entering the Dovey Valley and following it up to Cemmaes Road. Views up the valley towards **Mallwyd** can be enjoyed here before the road turns away on the A470 Newtown road to continue up the **Twymyn Valley** - an important road and rail route between west and central Wales. At **Llanbrynmair** the river turns south and tributaries join from the north and east. It is up one of the latter, the **River Laen**, that this tour

continues. The road climbs through a wooded gorge to the summit at **Talerddig**, a climb of some 700 ft from Machynlleth. Follow the broad **Carno Valley** through **Carno**. Continue through **Clatter** and **Pont-dolgoch** to reach **Caersws** on the River Severn. Continue on the A470, and after ¾ of a mile meet a T-junction and turn right on to the Llangurig road. Pass over a level crossing and follow the River Severn through **Llandinam**, the birthplace of **David Davies**, who did much to develop railways and coal-mining in Wales. His statue can be seen to the right on the way back to Llanidloes.

Llyn Clywedog

Competition

Win a Weekend For Two at The Metropole Hotel, Llandrindod Wells

This prize includes a weekend for two at the luxuriously appointed Metropole Hotel in the popular spa town of Llandrindod Wells. The prize will include accommodation, breakfast and dinner for two people for two nights and also free entry to the hotel's superb indoor leisure complex, comprising a 54ft swimming pool, sauna, steam room, whirl pool, exercise machines & beauty salon. The prize may be taken at any time during 1996, subject to availability at the hotel.

Your stay at this hotel will allow you to discover the picturesque town of Llandrindod Wells and the adjoining countryside of Radnorshire and the Brecon Beacons. To enter this competition, just complete the three questions below and return the entry form to Lily Publications by the 1st October 1995. The clues to the three questions set out below can be found by reading this guide.

1. What is the highest mountain in the Brecon Beacons?

Pen y Fan   Fan Nedd   Mynydd Troed

2. Where can the Lear's Magic Lantern Theatre be found?

Newtown   Brecon   Llandrindod Wells

3. When were the first of the Elan Valley Dams built?

1987   1892   1903

Name ....

Address...

....

Daytime Tel No.................................   **Evening Tel No**...........................

Competition Rules

All entrants to Brecon Beacons & Heart of Wales competition in 1995 must be received by the 1st October 1995. The competition is open to all UK and overseas residents over 18 years of age except for employers and employees of Lily Publications and the Metropole Hotel. All prizes are subject to availability. The prize includes dinner, bed and breakfast for two persons sharing a twin/double room for two nights. All extras such as drinks, telephone calls, travel etc must be paid for by the prize winner. The Editor's decision is final and no correspondence can be entered into. Entries must be posted on the coupon provided in this guide. One entry per family. Proof of postage will not be accepted as proof of receipt. Entrants are deemed to have accepted the rules and must agree to be bound by them. For further information regarding the competition you should write to Lily Publications, 12 Millfields Close, Kilgetty, Pembrokeshire SA68 0SA.

Accommodation & Eating Out

 YOUTH HOSTELS

Budget Accommodation in beautiful locations

▲ Individuals and families welcome

▲ Self-cater or try tasty meals

▲ Horseriding holidays (2, 5, 7 nights)

▲ From £5.95 per night

For a **free** leaflet: **01222-396766**

HOTELS AND GUEST HOUSES

ABERGAVENNY

PANTYBEILIAU HOUSE, Church Road, Gilwern. Country house accommodation set in 4 acres of grounds. Bed & breakfast available. Tel 01873 830264. See page 44

BRECON

THE BEACONS GUEST HOUSE, 16 Bridge Street, Brecon. Friendly, family run Georgian guesthouse close to town centre. Comfortable en suite rooms. Excellent home cooking. Bargain breaks available. Tel 01874 623339. See page 48

THE LANSDOWNE HOTEL & RESTAURANT, The Watton, Brecon. A carefully restored and furnished Georgian Hotel close to town centre and amenities. Warm, friendly atmosphere. Centrally heated, en suite bedrooms. Licensed restaurant. Tel 01874 623321. See page 50

OLD CASTLE FARM HOTEL, Llanfaes, Brecon. Situated in the Brecon Beacons National Park this 17th century farmhouse offers a wide range of rooms en suite. Bar. Lounge. 3 crowns WTB. Tel 01874 622120. See page 51

"THE OLD MILL" Felinfach, Brecon. Bed & Breakfast - 1 twin en-suite, 1 twin and 1 double both with vanity unit etc. Double twin min £27, max £30, single £16. Peacefully situated in its own grounds in the village of Felinfach, "The Old Mill" has a wealth of character. Friendly atmosphere, TV lounge, tea/coffee facilities. Brecon Beacons, Black Mountains nearby. Local pub within walking distance. Tel (01874) 625385.

PENPONT, Brecon. Idyllic setting on the banks of the River Usk.

Choice of bedrooms with en suite available. Beautiful grounds. Relaxed atmosphere. Tel 01874 636202. See page 49

PETERSTONE COURT, Llanhamlach, Brecon. Luxury hotel set in beautiful location. Wide range of rooms including suites and 4 poster bedroom. Restaurant. Croquet lawn. Leisure suite. Taste of Wales High Commendation. WTB 5 crowns de luxe.Tel 01874 665387. See page 47

UPPER CANTREF FARM & RIDING CENTRE, Cantref. Traditional farmhouse offering bed & breakfast and riding facilities. 2 crowns. Tel 01874 665223. See page 49

USK HOTEL, Talybont on Usk, Nr Brecon. Set on the edge of a small village in the heart of the Brecon Beacons National Park. Ideal centre for walking. All bedrooms with en suite facilities. Restaurant. Bar snacks. Tel 01874 87251. See page 74

THE WELLINGTON HOTEL, The Bulwark, Brecon. Friendly surroundings in which to enjoy your stay. Private bathrooms, colour TV, telephone, tea/coffee facilities. Tel 01874 625225 See page 52

BUILTH WELLS

DOL-ILYN-WYDD. 17th century farmhouse set in magnificent scenery. Warm welcome. Home cooking. WTB Highly commended 2 crowns. Tel 01982 553660. See page 97

THE WHITE HORSE HOTEL. Friendly hotel offering comfortable accommodation. All bedrooms en suite. Welcoming bars with good food. Tel 01982 553171. See page 97

CRICKHOWELL

DRAGON HOTEL, High Street, Crickhowell, NP8 1BE. Enjoy the relaxed atmosphere of our 18th century hotel, in the centre of picturesque Crickhowell, a friendly market town on the River Usk, where the Beacons meet the Black Mountains. Excellent for country activities/attractions and for outdoor enthusiasts. Individual en-suite rooms, some non-smoking. Bar/restaurant open daily. 'Taste of Wales' member. Tel (01873) 810362.

THE FARMERS ARMS, Cwmdu, Nr Crickhowell. Situated some 6 miles from the old town of Crickhowell in the heart of the Black Mountains. All rooms en suite. Good menu for all tastes, including vegetarian meals. 3 crowns WTB. Tel 01874 730464. See page 54

THE MANOR HOTEL, Brecon Road. This hotel stands in 14 acres of grounds with beautiful views looking towards the Usk Valley. En

Accommodation & Eating Out

suite bedrooms. Cocktail bar. Ballroom. A la carte restaurant. Pool and gymnasium. Tel 01873 810212. See page 55

HAY-ON-WYE

KILVERTS, The Bullring, Hay-on-Wye. Privately owned 11 bedroom hotel. All rooms en suite. Lively bar. A la carte restaurant. Award winning food cooked by chef. Tel 01497 820564. See page 101

THE SWAN AT HAY, Church Street, Hay-on-Wye. Georgian Hotel, family owned and managed. All rooms with bathroom en suite. A la carte restaurant. 4 crowns Highly Commended. Tel 01497 821188. See page 102

KNIGHTON

PILLETH COURT, Whitton, Knighton. Listed Elizabethan house tastefully furnished, still retaining wonderful character and atmosphere. All guest bedrooms with panoramic views. Wonderful centre for walking. WTB 2 crowns Highly Commended. Tel 01547 560272. See page 106

LLANDEILO

THE CAWDOR ARMS HOTEL AND RESTAURANT. Recently refurbished. High quality cuisine. Lunch and dinner and Sunday lunch available. Tel 01558 823500. See page 30

LLANDRINDOD WELLS

THE BELL COUNTRY INN. Centrally located in Mid Wales, with 9 luxury en suite bedrooms, 2 award winning restaurants. Ideal location for exploring Mid Wales. Tel 01597 823959. See page 108

GREENWAY MANOR HOTEL, Crossgates. Set in 10 acres of garden. Excellent food and accommodation within a warm and friendly atmosphere. Tel 01597 851230. See page 110

GRIFFIN LODGE HOTEL. Small licensed Victorian hotel situated in the heart of the town. Friendly atmosphere combined with good food. Well appointed rooms. Tel 01597 822342. See page 108

THE LLANERCH. 16th century inn set in own grounds near town centre. 11 en suite bedrooms. Excellent selection of meals and snacks. Traditional ales. Families welcome. Tel 01597 822086. See page 111

THE METROPOLE HOTEL. In the centre of Wales' premier spa town, our hotel offers modern comfortable facilities in Victorian surroundings. Swimming pool. Families welcome. Excellent cuisine. 4 crowns WTB. Tel 01597 823700. See page 108

LLANWRTYD WELLS

CARLTON HOUSE. Fully licensed small family run hotel standing at the gateway to the last unspoilt wilderness in Britain. Personal service offered to all our visitors. En suite accommodation available. For further details telephone 01591 610248. See page 112

LASSWADE COUNTRY HOUSE. Restaurant and en suite accommodation in a handsome Edwardian Country House set in Mid Wales countryside. Tel 01591 610515. See page 113

THE NEUADD ARMS HOTEL. First class hotel offering ideal base for walking, pony trekking, fishing holidays set in the heart of the Red Kite country. Tel 01591 610236. See page 113

MERTHYR TYDFIL

THE BAVERSTOCK HOTEL on the edge of the beautiful Brecon Beacons National Park. 3 star hotel with excellent cuisine. Well appointed en suite rooms. Freefone 0800 716010. See page 65

TY NEWYDD COUNTRY HOTEL, Penderyn Road, Hirwaun. At the foot of the Brecon Beacons. Grill and a la carte restaurant, banqueting suites, 29 en suite bedrooms. Tel 01685 813433 See page 65

RHAYADER

LIVERPOOL HOUSE, East Street, Rhayader. Bed, breakfast and optional evening meals. Most rooms en-suite. Secure private parking. WTB 3 crowns. Tel (01597) 810706. See page 118

Publisher's Note: Many of the premises listed under Eating Out offer accommodation

SELF-CATERING

BRECON BEACONS HOLIDAY COTTAGES. Wide selection of holiday cottages situated in the heart of the Brecon Beacons. Send for our colour brochure today. Tel 01874 87446. See inside front cover for advertisement.

GRANARY COTTAGES, Ystradgynwyn, Torpantau, CF4 2UT. Brecon Beacons 1,000ft. Between Talybont-on-Usk and Pontsticill. Wales Tourist Board Grade 4 and 5. Ideal location for walking and exploring. Children and dogs welcome. Enquiries and Brochure from Mrs Susan Williams, Tel (01685) 383358.

YOUTH HOSTELS

BRYN POETH UCHAF YOUTH HOSTEL, Hafod-y-Pant, Cynghordy, Llandovery, Dyfed SA20 0NB. Former farmhouse and barn in beautiful isolated location in the Cambrian mountains. Simple mountain hut-type accommodation, lit solely by gas with coal fire, self-catering facilities only. Wales Tourist Board approved. 22 beds. Separate, self-contained family annexe with bedroom, lounge, kitchen, shower and toilet facilities. Sleeps 4, can be hired. Tel (015505) 235.

CAPEL-Y-FFIN YOUTH HOSTEL, Capel-y-Ffin, Abergavenny,

Gwent, NP7 7NP. Converted farmhouse in peaceful Llanthony Valley providing dormitory accommodation, full meals service, showers and horseriding holidays. This Youth Hostel operates a no-smoking policy. Wales Tourist Board approved. 40 beds. Tel (01873) 890650.

GLASCWM YOUTH HOSTEL, The School, Glascwm, Llandrindod Wells, Powys, LD1 5SE. This former village school in the centre of the quiet hamlet of Glascwm provides basic accommodation with outside toilets. Self-catering facilities only, camping allowed in the grounds, parking nearby. Wales Tourist Board approved. 22 beds. Tel (01982) 570415.

LLANDDEUSANT YOUTH HOSTEL, The Old Red Lion, Llanddeusant, Llangadog, Dyfed, SA19 6UL. A former Inn adjacent to a 14th century church overlooking the magical Sawdde Valley. Ideal base for exploring the remote corners of the magnificent countryside. Comfortable accommodation with wash-basins in all rooms, family rooms, full heating, showers, self-catering facilities only, parking. Wales Tourist Board approved. 28 beds. The whole Youth Hostel can be hired out per night from 5 September 1995 to 31 March 1996. Tel (015505) 635 and 619.

LLWYN-Y-CELYN YOUTH HOSTEL, Libanus, Brecon, Powys, LD3 8NH. A traditional Welsh farmhouse set in 15 acres of woodland in the heart of the Brecon Beacons National Park. Ideal base for walks - from gentle strolls to spectacular ascents. Dormitory accommodation, full heating, showers, full meals service, nature trail, parking. Wales Tourist Board approved. 46 beds. Tel (01874) 624261.

TY'N-Y-CAEAU YOUTH HOSTEL, Groesffordd, Brecon, Powys, LD3 7SW. Large country house providing dormitory accommodation with excellent mountain views, only two and a half miles from the market town of Brecon. Full meals service, showers, extensive grounds, parking. Wales Tourist Board approved. 65 beds. Tel (01874) 665270.

YSTRADFELLTE YOUTH HOSTEL, Tai'r Heol, Ystradfellte, Aberdare, Mid Glamorgan, CF44 9JF. Three 17th century cottages make up this small rural Youth Hostel only half a mile south of the village of Ystradfellte, in the heart of waterfall and caving country. Dormitory accommodation, showers, self-catering facilities only, parking. Wales Tourist Board approved. 28 beds. Tel (01639) 720301.

CARAVAN AND CAMPING

BRYNICH CARAVAN PARK, Brecon. Easy access to quiet, beautifully maintained 15 acre flat site with panoramic views. Cleanliness a priority. Adventure playground. Friendly atmosphere. Tel 01874 623325. See page 52

GRAWEN CARAVAN AND CAMPING PARK, Cwm Taff, Merthyr Tydfil. Situated in picturesque mountain position. Open April to October. All modern facilities. Tel 01685 723740. See page 67

LAKESIDE CARAVAN AND CAMPING PARK, Llangorse, Brecon. Stay in our modern holiday caravans or bring your own tent or tourer. Cafe on site. Swimming pool. Ideal location to explore the beautiful Llangorse Lake area. Tel 01874 658226. See page 60

LLYNFI HOLIDAY PARK, Llangorse, Brecon. Situated in 17 acres in the heart of the Brecon Beacons, near Llangorse Lake. All facilities available. Licensed bar. Own launching jetty for boats. Tel 01874 84283. See page 60

RIVERSIDE INTERNATIONAL CARAVAN & CAMPING, Bronllys, Talgarth, Nr Brecon. Modern caravan park situated on the edge of the Brecon Beacons National Park. Leisure centre with swimming pool. Bar and restaurant. Open Easter to October. Tel 01874 711320. See page 74

EATING OUT

CAMDEN ARMS, Brecon. 16th century inn offering good Welsh cooking for everyone. Bar meals. Real ale. Sunday lunches. Children welcome. Tel 01874 89282. See page 51

CANTREF INN, Brecon Road, Abergavenny. Family run pub with wide selection of Whitbread beers and real ales. Extensive menu at reasonable prices. Tel 01873 855827. See page 44

THE CASTLE COACHING INN, Trecastle, Brecon. Once a coaching Inn on the route from London to Fishguard, open fires, first class food, good sized bedrooms with private bathrooms, all facilities. Tel 01874 636354 See page 75

THE COACH HOUSE, Craig-y-Nos. Located in beautiful position with craft shop and tea rooms. Coaches welcome with prior booking. Home made food. Tel 01639 730767. See page 10

CORDELL COUNTRY INN, Blacnavin Road, Govilon, Nr Abergavenny. Pleasant country inn offering selection of bar meals including vegetarian menu. Bed & breakfast. Traditional Sunday lunch. Children welcome. Tel 01873 830436. See page 43

THE DROVERS ARMS, Llandrindod Wells. Traditional Welsh pub with real ale. High quality a la carte bar meals. Sunday lunches. Egon Ronay recommended. Tel 01597 822508. See page 111

THE DROVERS RESTAURANT, Llandovery. Situated in the heart of Llandovery town offering a wide selection of meals for all tastes. Tel 01550 21115. See page 32

EAGLE HOTEL, New Radnor. Friendly coaching inn in picturesque village. Comfortable accommodation available. Excellent, reasonably priced home cooking, including vegetarian meals. Open all day. Tel 01544 350208. See page 115

THE FFOREST INN, Llanfihangel-Nant-Melan, New Radnor. Centuries of old drovers have been stopping at this point. Fine range of

Accommodation & Eating Out

traditional food all prepared on the premises. Guest cask ales. WTB 2 crowns. Tel 01554 350246. See page 115

GRASSHOPPERS BAR/CAFE, Beaufort Street, Crickhowell and St John's Square, Abergavenny. Both our premises offer a wide variety of traditional food and ales. Always a friendly and lively atmosphere. Tel 01873 810402/01873 854939. See page 56

THE HARP INN, Glasbury on Wye, Nr Hay on Wye. Enjoy home cooked food and a pint of real ale beside the River Wye. Vegetarian meals available. Welsh village pub of the year in 1993. Tel 01497 847373. See page 101

HUNDRED HOUSE INN, Bleddfa, Knighton. Friendly welcome awaits you at this country inn. Traditional ales, bar meals. Families welcome. Sunday lunches. Tl 01547 81333. See page 106

LA BRASERIA RESTAURANT & FORTUNA WINE BAR, 22a High Street, Brecon. Tel 01874 611313.

THE NANTYFFIN CIDER MILL INN & DINING ROOM, Crickhowell. Popular food pub with attractive surroundings. Wide choice of food. Keg beers and decent ciders. Disabled facilities. Tel 01873 810775. See page 54

THE NEW INN, Bwlch, Nr Brecon. Good food and fine ales together with a friendly atmosphere is the boast of the New Inn. Ideal base from which to explore the Brecon Beacons. Tel 01874 730215. See page 53

THE NEW INN, Llanbadarn Fynydd, Nr Llandrindod Wells. Wide choice of meals offered at this beautiful 16th century inn. Traditional ales. Families welcome. Tel 01597 840378. See page 111

OLD PANDY INN, Hereford Road, Pandy, Abergavenny. Unique range of real ales. All food home cooked. Bar Snacks. Traditional Sunday Lunch. Patio Garden. Large car park. **Saffron's Restaurant.** Oriental, Thai, Indian, Mexican and inspiring English dishes. Tel 01873 890208. See page 44

PEPPERS RESTAURANT, The Watton, Brecon. Wide range of quality cooked meals and snacks. Sunday lunches. Vegetarians and children catered for. Tel 01874 622526. See page 49

THE PLOUGH INN, Rhosmaen. Bar meals and afternoon teas available in our Towy Lounge. Restaurant for lunch and dinner. Traditional family Sunday lunches available. Tel 01558 823431. See page 30

THE RADNOR ARMS, Llowes, Hereford. Traditional inn offering wide selection of lunches and dinners. Vegetarian. Real ale. Large wine list. Garden. Tel 01497 847460. See page 102

THE RHYDSPENCE INN, Whitney-on-Wye, Hereford. Set in the heart of Kilvert country this traditional inn offers 2 attractive bars. Bar meals and snacks available. Restaurant. Accommodation available.

English Tourist Board 3 crowns. Good Beer and Good Pub Guides recommended. Tel 01497 831262. See page 102

STONECROFT INN, Llanwrtyd Wells. Traditional country pub with real ales and good food. Bed & breakfast available. Riverside garden. Tel 01591 610322. See page 114

TAI'R BULL INN, Libanus, Brecon. Small friendly inn situated close to the Mountain Centre in the Brecon Beacons. Accommodation available. Bar and restaurant meals. Tel 01874 625849. See page 58

THE TROUT INN AND RESTAURANT, Llanwrtyd Wells. Lovely village pub offering a wide range of bar snacks. Cosy dining room. Accommodation available. Wonderful location to explore Mid Wales. Tel 01591 620235. See page 113

YE OLDE RED LION HOTEL, Queen Victoria Street, Tredegar. A warm Welsh welcome is always found at our hotel. Traditional bar. Accommodation. Tel 01495 724449. See page 67

ACKNOWLEDGEMENTS

My thanks are due to John Norris, Diane Russell, Mike Wilson, C.S. Moscrop, Roger Stevens and Sue Parrott for their contributions. I would also like to thank again those many people who have helped in the production of this first edition, notably Jane Lewis (Brecknock Council); Mary Price (Radnor Council); Trevor Barrett; Roger Ferris and the staff of Haven Colourprint; John Sidney (Harcourt Litho); Ian Smith (Bézier Design), Marilyn Gardner (Waterfront Graphics); Pat & Geoff Somner of Lily Publications; Rhys Jones of the Wales Tourist Board. Finally, a big thanks again to David Lemon and all the advertisers.

Tourist Information Centres

Open all year

Hay-on-Wye, Powys HR3 5AE
TIC, The Crafts Centre, Oxford Road.
Tel (01497) 820144.

Knighton, Powys LD7 1EW
TIC, Offa's Dyke Association,
The Old School.
Tel (01547) 528753.

Llandrindod Wells, Powys LD1 6AA
TIC, Radnor District Council,
The Old Town Hall.
Tel (01597) 822600.

Machynlleth, Powys SY20 8EE
TIC, Canolfan Owain Glyndwr,
Maengwyn Street.
Tel (01654) 702401.

Merthyr Tydfil, Mid Glamorgan CF47 8AU
TIC, 14a Glebeland Street.
Tel (01685) 78884.

Newport, Gwent NP9 1HZ
TIC, Newport Museum & Art Gallery,
John Frost Sq
Tel (01633) 842962.

Welshpool, Powys SY21 7DD
TIC, Vicarage Gardens Car Park.
Tel (01938) 52043.

Open Easter to end of September

Abercraf, Powys SA9 1GJ
TIC, Dan-yr-Ogof Showcaves,
Upper Swansea Valley.
Tel (01639) 730284.

Abergavenny, Gwent NP7 4HH
TIC, Swan Meadow, Cross Street.
Tel (01873) 77588.

Brecon, Powys LD3 9DA
TIC, Castle Market Car Park.
Tel (01874) 2485.

Brecon, Powys LD3 7DF
Brecon Beacons National Park Centre,
Watton Mount.
Tel (01874) 4437.

Builth Wells, Powys LD2 3BL
TIC, Groe Car Park.
Tel (01982) 553307.

Chepstow, Gwent NP6 5LH
TIC, The Gatehouse, High Street.
Tel (012912) 3772.

Elan Valley, Powys LD6 5HP
Elan Valley Visitor Centre
Tel (01597) 810898.

Llanfyllin, Powys SY22 5DB
TIC, Council Offices
Tel (01691) 848868.

Llanidloes, Powys SY18 6ES
TIC, Longbridge Street.
Tel (015512) 2605.

Newtown, Powys SY16 2PW
TIC, Central Car Park.
Tel (01686) 625580.

Presteigne, Powys
TIC, Market Hall.
Tel (01544) 260193.

Rhayader, Powys LD6 5AB
TIC, The Old Swan.
Tel (01597) 810591.

Other useful addresses

Brecon Beacons National Park,
7 Glamorgan Street,
Brecon, Powys LD3 7DP.
Tel Brecon (01874) 4437.

Brecon Beacons Mountain Centre,
Nr Libanus,
Brecon,
Powys LD3 8ER.
Tel Brecon (01874) 3366.

Brecknock Naturalists' Trust,
c/o Chapel House,
Llechfaen,
Brecon LD3 7SP,
Tel Llanfrynach (0187 486) 688.

Council for National Parks,
45 Shelton Street,
London WC2 9HJ.
Tel 071 240 3603.

Countryside Commission,
Office for Wales,
Ladywell House,
Newtown,
Powys SY16 1RD.
Tel Newtown (01686) 26799

Forestry Commission,
Victoria House,
Victoria Terrace,
Aberystwyth,
Dyfed SY23 2DQ.
Tel Aberystwyth (01970) 612367.

Wales Tourist Board,
PO Box 1,
Cardiff CF1 2XN.
Tel Cardiff (01222) 27281.

Index

Numbers in *italics* refer to photographs